M.gft

CHICAGO
METROPOLIS 2020

A PROJECT OF THE
COMMERCIAL CLUB OF CHICAGO
IN ASSOCIATION WITH THE
AMERICAN ACADEMY OF ARTS
AND SCIENCES

THE CHICAGO PLAN FOR THE
TWENTY-FIRST CENTURY

CHICAGO METROPOLIS
2020

ELMER W. JOHNSON

WITH A FOREWORD BY DONALD L. MILLER

The University of Chicago Press   Chicago and London

This publication is underwritten in part by R.R. Donnelley & Sons Company.

The University of Chicago Press, Chicago 60637
The University of Chicago Press, Ltd., London
Printed in the United States of America
10 09 08 07 06 05 04 03 02 01   1 2 3 4 5
ISBN 0-226-40200-2

Library of Congress Cataloging-in-Publication Data
Johnson, Elmer W.
    Chicago metropolis 2020 : the Chicago plan for the
twenty-first century / Elmer W. Johnson ; With a Foreword
by Donald L. Miller
      p. cm.
    "A project of the Commercial Club of Chicago in
association with the American Academy of Arts and
Sciences."
    ISBN 0-226-40200-2 (hardcover : alk. paper)
    1. City planning—Illinois—Chicago Metropolitan
Area. 2. Chicago Metropolitan Area (Ill.)—Economic
conditions—21st century. I. Commercial Club of Chicago.
II. American Academy of Arts and Sciences. III. Title.
HT168.C5 J64 2001
307.1´216´0977311—dc21   2001001009

∞ The paper used in this publication meets the minimum requirements of the American National Standard for Information Sciences—Permanence of Paper for Printed
Library Materials, ANSIZ39.48-1992.

Participants

THE COMMERCIAL CLUB OF CHICAGO

The Commercial Club of Chicago was founded in 1877 in order "to advance the public welfare and the commercial interests of metropolitan Chicago by co-operative effort, social intercourse, and a free interchange of views." Election to membership is "limited to residents of the Chicago metropolitan area who shall be deemed qualified by reason of their personality, general reputation, position in their business or profession, and service in the public welfare." The Civic Committee, whose responsibilities are to consider needs and plans for the development of the Chicago metropolitan area, is appointed annually by the Chairman of the Club.

THE AMERICAN ACADEMY OF ARTS AND SCIENCES

The American Academy, founded in 1780, is an international learned society with a three-fold mission: to recognize excellence in science and scholarship, the arts, and public affairs; to promote the life of the mind and the dissemination of knowledge; and to bring together the resources of the intellectual community to address issues in the public interest. Its headquarters are located in Cambridge, Massachusetts, and it maintains regional centers at the University of Chicago and the University of California, Irvine.

PROJECT DIRECTOR

Elmer W. Johnson is President and Trustee of the Aspen Institute, a partner in the law firm of Kirkland and Ellis, and a former Executive Vice President and Director of General Motors Corporation. He is a Fellow of the American Academy of Arts and Sciences and has been a member of the Commercial Club of Chicago since 1978. He is also a member of its Civic Committee.

GRAPHICS COMMITTEE

The Graphics Committee, which oversaw the creation and commission of maps and illustrations for the book, consisted of Chairman Laurence O. Booth, Lawrence Christmas, Michael Conzen, and Patrick Whitney. Nancy Canfield served as consultant to the committee.

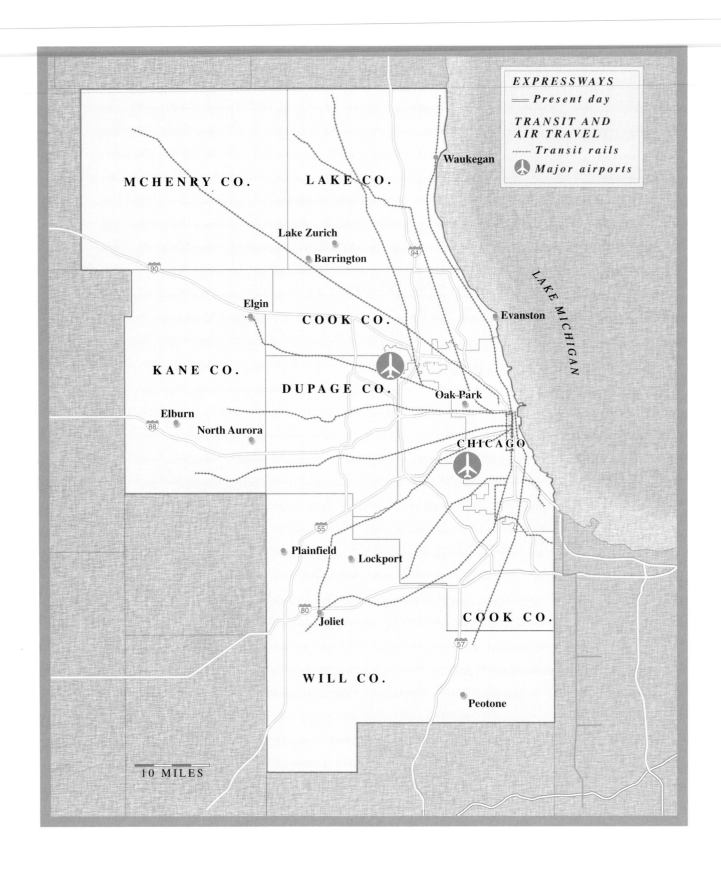

EXPRESSWAYS
—— *Present day*

TRANSIT AND
AIR TRAVEL
⊢⊢⊢ *Transit rails*
✈ *Major airports*

LAKE MICHIGAN

MCHENRY CO.

LAKE CO.

Waukegan

Lake Zurich

Barrington

94

Elgin

COOK CO.

Evanston

KANE CO.

DUPAGE CO.

Oak-Park

Elburn

88

North Aurora

CHICAGO

55

Plainfield

Lockport

80

Joliet

COOK CO.

57

WILL CO.

Peotone

10 MILES

Contents

THE CITY OF CHICAGO.

"Bird's-eye view" of Chicago by Currier & Ives, 1874. This lithograph was revised in 1892 for the World's Columbian Exposition.

Foreword

Donald L. Miller

The Metropolis 2020 Plan positions Chicago for the unprecedented challenges of the next century. It is a visionary strategy that calls on Chicago to become what it was a century ago, one of the most innovative cities in the world in business, technology, and urban reform, a place people visited to catch a glimpse of the metropolitan future.

Prepared and sponsored by the Commercial Club of Chicago, one of the city's oldest civic organizations, and written by Elmer W. Johnson, the Metropolis Plan is an ingenious blend of idealism and pragmatism. And it is a workable plan because it arises from a close-textured understanding of the metropolitan region it proposes to reshape: an understanding of its history and heritage as well as its present problems and possibilities.

The Metropolis Plan is a characteristically Chicago form of planning that seeks to harmonize two seemingly warring impulses: privatism and public control. The marriage of these two impulses was one of the signal achievements of the Burnham Plan of 1909, which was also sponsored by the Commercial Club.

The recommendations of the new plan are not mere urban cosmetic; they are substantial and are sure to be challenged by those metropolitan groups who prefer things the way they are. This is not, however, a dreamy work of urban prophecy. It is a plan that aims high, but it is informed by the kind of hardheaded practicality Chicago has long been known for.

The Metropolis Plan mirrors the Burnham Plan of 1909 in its audacious metropolitan scope and in its challenge to the business community to take the lead in urban reconstruction, working in partnership with city government. Yet it recognizes that Chicago in the year 2000 is a greatly different place than Carl Sandburg's big-shouldered city of 1900, and that these changes call for social policies bolder than those proposed by the master builder Daniel Hudson Burnham and his assistant Edward H. Bennett.

It is, however, the "Chicagoness" of the new plan, its deep-layered understanding of the character and history of the city that gives it its strength. One of the great themes of Chicago's history is the ongoing battle between growth and control, restraint and opportunity, privatism and the public good. Nineteenth-century Chicago, the world's newest big city, seemed to have sprung up spontaneously, without planning or social foresight, a pure product of ungoverned capitalism. Yet this city of unbounded growth undertook some of the most ambitious public improvement projects of the modern urban age, including the Burnham Plan, which was adopted by city government and has guided downtown development throughout most of the twentieth century.

As the Metropolis Plan recognizes, Chicago has worked best, has got more things done and done well, when the private and public sectors have worked in harmony, and when business interests have channeled their capital and capacities into civic improvement. In Chicago, urban planning has historically tried to tame, but never shackle, what is perhaps the city's outstanding attribute: its ferocious entrepreneurial energy.

Chicago was built for business. It was the creation of what John Maynard Keynes called those beasts of capitalism: risk-taking and innovation. It embodied better than any other place the brutal and inventive vitality of nineteenth-century capitalism. Industrial capitalism's supreme urban creation, Chicago rose from mud hole to metropolis, from desolate frontier fur trading post to skyscraper city of over a million people, in a mere sixty years.

No American city, not even New York, had grown so fast, and growth brought both opportunities and problems. Chicago's meatpacking mills and mail-order houses were marvels of machine-age efficiency. And in the 1890s, Chicago's downtown was a technological wonder, with streets lit by electricity, serviced by rapid-running electric streetcars, and lined by solid rows of office skyscrapers, tradition-shattering buildings that altered the course of architecture.

Daniel Burnham's Chicago was known for its brassy self-confidence. It was a city that took on big challenges and got things done. Its citizens had an invincible confidence in the possibilities of the place and in their own possibilities as well, for Chicago, with its vast, vertically organized corporations, was one of the great opportunity centers in the world, drawing workers from all over the globe.

A city without restricting traditions or an entrenched elite, it encouraged fresh ideas in business, architecture, urban reform, and the arts. It drew to it some of the outstanding innovators of the age, from Frank Lloyd Wright to Jane Addams to Philip Armour.

But the dynamic capitalism that created this magnet metropolis also turned it, for a time, into an ecological wasteland and a place of staggering income disparities and ethnic and racial discord.

In the 1840s and 1850s, Chicagoans literally drank their own sewage, as the Chicago River, the city's waste dump, flowed into Lake Michigan, the source of the city's water supply. Predictably, Chicago was struck by a succession of cholera epidemics; one of them killed 6 percent of the city's people.

For years, Chicago's city government, controlled by the business barons who built the city, refused to do anything about this alarming public health problem, unwilling to tax themselves to save their city. Nor would they place social controls on the railroads that were the foundation of Chicago's prosperity. Unlike New York, where citizen protests had led to legislation prohibiting railroad locomotives from entering the congested center of Manhattan, in freewheeling Chicago the railroads steamed into the heart of town, creating tremendous smoke and noise pollution, and killing or mangling an average of two persons a day at unprotected rail crossings. As one foreign visitor marveled: "It is cheaper to kill people than to elevate the railways, and human life in Chicago is nothing compared with money."

Nineteenth-century Chicago was the American Manchester. Here the new industrial order was on display in its full splendor and squalor. A commercial colossus, it was also one of the ugliest cities in America, and one of the most dangerous to human life, as well.

Just before the Civil War, outraged Chicago citizens finally forced city leaders to address the water pollution problem. Led by the city's founding father, William Butler Ogden, these business titans acted with surprising audacity, funding a series of sewage reforms that led, eventually, to the building of the Chicago Sanitary and Ship Canal in the 1890s. This enormous public works project, on the scale of the Suez Canal, reversed the flow of the Chicago River, carrying sewage away from Lake Michigan. Once the unhealthiest city in the nation, Chicago became almost at once the healthiest.

And Ellis Chesbrough, the Boston engineer who was brought in to build a new water supply and sewage system, lifted Chicago out of the mud and swampy soil that were breeding places for cholera. Contractors hired by Chesbrough, including the future railroad king George Pullman, raised up the entire downtown by as much as ten feet in places, jacking up entire rows of buildings and placing dredged soil from the river bottom underneath them.

The raising of the city and the reversal of the river were two of the outstanding engineering projects of the age. They gave Chicago its reputation as a city that could accomplish almost anything, a reputation enhanced by the complete rebuilding of the downtown, in less than a decade, after the Great Fire of 1871.

Economic innovation continued to accompany urban innovation in the post-fire city. In its gigantic meatpacking plants—perfectly synchronized killing and cutting machines—Chicago invented the world's first assembly line, a new way of making things that transformed the world. Later, Henry Ford claimed that he got the inspiration for his automobile assembly line during a visit to the Chicago stockyards. Modern mass production was born, not in Detroit, but in the blood and stink of the Chicago meat mills.

Foreign observers were fascinated by the businessmen who ran these mass-production lines. But the great size and speed of these operations, their ruthless cost cutting, and the almost total absence of government regulation led to scandalously lax health standards and to brutal labor exploitation. By turning Packingtown into a fortress of oppression, meat barons like Philip Armour made Chicago the national center not only of industrial ingenuity but also of industrial violence.

By the late 1880s, Chicago's leading capitalists had become convinced that the town they had helped to build with their sweat and money would never be a world capital the like of London or Paris unless it began to discipline its cyclonic growth and alter its image and appearance. Chicago had just been rocked by a succession of violent labor upheavals that brought the city close to social revolution. At the same time, the business elite had lost control of the political system to ward bosses sympathetic to the rising expectations of the city's ethnic neighborhoods. All this might have produced a crisis of confidence. But for Chicago's business leaders, challenge and conflict had always been sources of energy and opportunity. Adversity and opposition had drawn them more closely together in tremendous civic endeavors, like the river reversal and the raising of the city—projects designed to ensure uninterrupted commercial growth. This was the unstoppable city that had seen its very destruction by fire as an opportunity for regeneration.

In preparing to host a world's fair in 1893 that would showcase their city, Chicago's business elite carried through a civic renaissance unparalleled, up to then, in the history of American cities. They built several superb libraries, a world-class center of learning in the University of Chicago (with the help of an injection of Rockefeller money), an impressive new museum for the Art Institute on Michigan Avenue, and a civic center for the performing arts, Dankmar Adler and Louis Sullivan's Auditorium Building. They also expanded Chicago's impressive system of parks and carriage runs.

Burnham's Chicago Plan of 1909 was the crowning achievement of this civic awakening. America's first metropolitan plan—a plan encompassing both the city and its surrounding regions—gave Chicago its peerless lakefront, established the Parisian-boulevard character of Michigan Avenue, and protected from development forest land on the periphery of the city.

The Burnham Plan was the first direct challenge to Chicago's reckless growth. "Men are becoming convinced that the formless growth of the city is neither economical nor satisfactory," Burnham wrote. Chicagoans needed to think less about how their city was growing and more about how they were living. "It was time," he proclaimed, "to bring order out of the chaos incident to rapid growth."

A number of nineteenth-century Chicago novels are about the irreconcilable conflict in the city between art and commerce. But Burnham and his closest supporters in the business community, men like Charles Hutchinson, the financier who headed the Art Institute, combined their cultural reformism with pride in Chicago's business accomplishments. Chicago could be culturally transformed, they were convinced, without challenging its commitment to commerce. "The past shows plainly enough," Burnham declared, in his florid manner, "that the great flowers of fine arts are born on the stalk of commercial supremacy. It has been so from Athens to Chicago."

The Burnham Plan, a businessman's vision of city reform, made no provision for the needs of blighted, inner-city neighborhoods. As Elmer Johnson indicates, it was primarily about urban beautification. The Metropolis 2020 Plan, on the other hand, "is about the quality of life and equity of opportunity that will be required to assure the economic vitality of the Chicago region." As such, it represents a considerable enlargement of the social awareness of many of the city's commercial leaders. Yet both the Burnham and the Metropolis plan do share a common concern: suburban sprawl.

The Burnham Plan attacked unregulated suburban growth, then in its nascent stage, and called for the orderly development of suburbs and the preservation of green space under the auspices of a regionwide metropolitan council. These recommendations anticipate those of the new plan. While Johnson and his Commercial Club associates favor local over regional government, they urge coordinate action to address problems that traverse municipal boundaries, such as traffic congestion, pollution, and persistent housing segregation.

On the occasion of the presentation of the plan to city government, at a Commercial Club dinner in January 1910, Alderman Bernard Snow, a member of the Commercial Club, had this to say: "One of the clearest lessons which is taught in this magnificent volume, is the absolute necessity of the consolidation of all forms of government, not merely within Chicago but within the territory laying about and actually a part of the metropolitan territory of Chicago."

Snow then called for a program to eradicate slum housing. "Proper housing," he said, "[is] the birthright of humanity. If we permit Chicago's slums to resemble those of Calcutta, we must accept the responsibility for the inevitable result." Strong words, words not found in the published version of the Burnham Plan, but a statement of civic purpose that Burnham did include, in his own handwriting, in the unpublished draft of his plan. These passages, stricken from the published plan, call for a redefinition of the city's responsibility for providing human services, including daycare centers, research hospitals, and better designed public schools and playgrounds.

There is no extant documentation indicating why these deletions were made. But Burnham, a master salesman as well as a master builder, surely worried about selling ideas to businessmen for the social, as well as physical, reconstruction of Chicago.

The new plan has no such reservations: it calls for bold action on a broad front to address the city's social inequities, especially its scandalous "hyperconcentration" and isolation of poor people of color.

Daniel Burnham was an urban imperialist who dreamed of making Chicago "a greater city than any existing at the present time." Growth, he insisted, must not be stopped; but it had to be shaped by positive human action in order to improve the quality of life in every area of the metropolitan region, not just the most privileged ones. In its emphasis on inter-regional cooperation to end "destructive competition" among greater Chicago's 267 municipalities and 1,276 local government bodies, the Metropolis 2020 Plan builds on the solid legacy of the Burnham Plan.

A self-made millionaire architect, Burnham did not see his plan as either a challenge to, or a rejection of, free-market capitalism. He and his supporters in the corporate community saw patronage of the arts and urban beautification as ways of enhancing their own fame and making Chicago a more pleasing and profitable place to do business.

The Metropolis Plan strikes a similar note. As Chicago plans for the twenty-first century, it cannot afford to lose its competitive edge. "Our region," Johnson writes, "must provide an environment . . . that serves as an incubator of new enterprises." Nor, he argues implicitly, can Chicago allow itself to become what parts of New York City have already become, a government-sustained economy built on paternalism, the idea that the poor cannot survive without the help of municipal bureaucrats. Such an economy will only exacerbate the economic inequality that is perhaps the single most dangerous problem confronting Chicago and other big cites. Inner-city America will never be economically integrated until it fully participates in and benefits from the wealth-creating market economy. The Metropolis Plan moves in the right direction by suggesting creative ways to get money into the hands of disadvantaged urban communities that can use it to become self-supporting.

Chicago's history reminds us that what will count in the future are what counted in the past: hard work, thrift, tenacity, family solidarity, and community cooperation. No empowerment is more effective than self-empowerment. That is the clear, insistent message of the Commercial Club's metropolitan report.

But the poor will need help, because some of their problems are the result of deliberate public policy that encourages racial and ethnic segregation, in the suburbs as well as the inner city. Changing these policies, Johnson argues, is not just the humane thing to do; it is the sensible thing to do if Chicago is to have a pool of stable and skilled workers capable of luring new knowledge-based businesses to the city.

Poverty in Chicago today, we need to remember, is hugely different than it was in Daniel Burnham's time. When young Theodore Dreiser walked the streets of Chicago in the 1880s, he noticed that even in the most squalid slums there was no spirit of despair. Instead he found hope, eagerness, and desire. Most immigrants (Chicago was then an overwhelmingly white city) were unskilled, but Chicago's roaring industrial plants were creating jobs at an incredible rate. And the working poor had an inexpensive and efficient mass transit to get them to these jobs.

When immigrants accumulated enough savings, they moved along transit corridors to new low-income housing on the edge of the city, where speculative builders like Samuel Eberly Gross, a local housing "impresario," put up tens of thousands of inexpensive houses. In this earlier Chicago, working people were ever on the move, in search of new opportunities.

Chicago was doing then what Jane Jacobs says all healthy cities do. "A metropolitan economy, if it is working well," Jacobs writes, "is constantly transforming many poor people into middle-class people. Cities don't lure the middle class, they create it."

Today, good jobs are moving to the suburbs, and as the new plan points out, there is no easy way for many inner-city poor people—the great majority of them black and Hispanic—to get to them, except by automobile. Yet fully a third of Chicago's households do not own a car. This is a formula for social disaster.

One of the great strengths of the Metropolis Plan is that it connects job training with a transportation and housing policy that, together, promise to do for today's upward-bound urbanites what low-skilled industrial jobs and cheap mass transit did for immigrants a century ago. The Metropolis Plan sees the entire Chicago region as an interconnected ecosystem and presages a return to the symbiotic relationship between city and suburb that existed in the age of the electric streetcar. At the end of the nineteenth century, mass transit promoted, simultaneously, the growth of the central city and of the suburbs, and pulled them together into an organic bond. But with the coming of the automobile, urban transportation corridors became escapeways from the city, not linkages to it. And the linear logic of the railroad suburbs—village-like places situated along the tracks at decent intervals, with natural greenbelts between them—was broken, giving rise to the formless "spread city."

Cars are indispensable to modern life, as Elmer Johnson, a former automobile executive, points out. But Johnson argues that too many cars and trucks in one place can have a ruinous impact on the great contributors to urban vitality: pedestrian concentration and the swift movement of people and products.

AT THIS STAGE, the Metropolis Plan is a document for discussion and debate. What gives hope for its implementation is Chicago's historic capacity for regeneration. Today, there is a lot of talk about corporate adaptability. The thriving companies in the global economy will be those that adapt most creatively to new challenges, it is argued. But the cities that capture these adaptable corporations will be cities that are themselves adaptable, able to reconfigure themselves to take advantages of new global opportunities.

Chicago has done that already, reinventing itself at least three times: after the Great Fire of 1871, in the wake of the Burnham Plan, and in the 1950s, during the administration of Richard J. Daley. The sustaining force of this historic process of renewal is Chicago's strongest spiritual asset: its swaggering self-confidence.

This cannot be underestimated as a propellant of economic and civic revitalization. As historian David S. Landes writes in *The Wealth and Poverty of Nations,* his important book about why some nations create great wealth and others do not: "In this world, the optimists have it, not because they are always right, but because they are positive. Even when they're wrong, they are positive, and that is the way of achievement, correction, improvement, and success. Educated, eyes-open optimism pays. Pessimism can only offer the empty consolation of being right."

Daniel Burnham was a convert to what he called the Chicago Spirit, which is nothing more than David Landes's secular optimism. "This spirit still exists," Burnham wrote. "It is present among us and is *impelling* us to larger and better achievements for the public good."

This is the Daniel Burnham we rarely hear about, the urban idealist who refused payment for his work on the Chicago Plan and who could write with unrestrained passion about his city. "To love one's city and have a part in its advancement and improvement is the highest privilege and duty of a citizen."

At a time when most American cities were burdened with seemingly unmanageable problems, Burnham and his Commercial Club associates insisted that the multiplying problems of the industrial city could be met and mastered by regionwide cooperation. For them, trend was not destiny.

This same civic optimism, and with it a far deeper commitment to the disadvantaged than we find in the Burnham Plan, undergirds the Metropolis 2020 Plan. But it is a new Chicago the plan describes and seeks to change. The Metropolis Plan is an effort to adjust urban planning to the challenges of the postindustrial age. Power and population in the modern city have shifted tremendously to the suburbs; and the gigantic corporations that made Chicago a world leader of industrial change are giving way to smaller, more adaptive firms, knowledge-based concerns linked to one another by modern information technologies.

But some things about cities never change. Great cities like Chicago and New York, with their favorable locations, are not ordained by geography. "They are," as Jane Jacobs writes, "wholly existential," creations of hard, human effort. And they are the products, not of rigid master plans, but of an ongoing and uneasy balance between order and energy, restraint and opportunity, public regulation and private initiative. They are places of messy vitality, known for both their cupidity and their surging civic spirit.

This supple plan, a set of informed suggestions, not a blueprint for an ideal city, promises to narrow economic inequities and right the social balance in Chicago while keeping it a capitalist powerhouse, a city energized by crisis, contention, and competition. It offers no easy answers, no sweeping panaceas. Even its most modest suggestions will be difficult to implement in the raucous give-and-take of Chicago politics. But it is an inspiring guide for the new century, as people everywhere seek ways to build and maintain cities that retain their humanity without losing their energy.

Acknowledgments

To achieve the best possible conditions of living for all the residents of metropolitan Chicago, we who live in this region must carry out two tasks simultaneously. First, we must continue to take seriously our lives as members of particular localities within the region, building stronger communities and neighborhoods. Second, we must learn to do something well that we have so far been doing only in fits and starts, namely, we must think and work together as a region. Chicago Metropolis 2020 (the plan) focuses mainly on the second of these two tasks.

The subject of "regionalism" has been around for a long time, and the Commercial Club of Chicago is deeply indebted to those who have focused on this subject over the last few decades. In the 1970s, for example, Portland, Oregon, embarked on innovative programs to create urban growth boundaries and curtail sprawl, and the Twin Cities in Minnesota began to create mechanisms for tax-base sharing in that metropolitan region. The Urban Land Institute has focused for many years on the policy implications of the changing land-use patterns in metropolitan America. A few years ago, the Regional Plan Association for the New York–New Jersey–Connecticut metropolitan area issued a 250-page document entitled "A Region at Risk." It sets forth a comprehensive plan for rebuilding the quality of life and the economic competitiveness of this large metropolitan area. Earlier, the Bank of America and certain other organizations issued a study on the costs of urban and suburban sprawl in California.

In our own metropolitan area, two organizations deserve special mention. First, the Metropolitan Planning Council has taken the lead (together with the Northeastern Illinois Planning Commission) over the last decade in making the case for regional cooperation and identifying the critical issues. And the Federal Reserve Bank of Chicago for many years has convened forums and conducted studies on the concerns of the larger region. The knowledge and expertise of their staffs have been indispensable to the development of this plan. Among the many other organizations who are devoted to various aspects of the region's economic, environmental, and social well-being, and whose leaders have given wise counsel to the development of this document, are Business and Professional People for the Public Interest; the Center for Neighborhood Technology; Chicago United, Inc.; the Civic Federation; the Leadership Council for Metropolitan Open Communities; the Local Initiatives Support Corporation; and the Environmental Law and Policy Center.

We have greatly benefited from consultation with many scholars at universities in the region: DePaul University, Northwestern University, Roosevelt University, the University of

Chicago, and the University of Illinois at Chicago. Some of these institutions have well-established centers for urban studies.

Most of the issues addressed in the document have a strong moral component—for example, values concerning equality of opportunity for education and employment, fiscal equity, household mobility, public housing for the poor, and neighborhood quality. The Club is indebted to church, civic, and labor leaders for raising people's consciousness of these values, which are at the very heart of this plan. Some of these leaders have formed organizations within the last five years to address regional issues from a moral perspective—organizations such as the Metropolitan Alliance of Congregations, United Power for Action, and Protestants for the Common Good.

We would be remiss if we did not take notice of the many efforts in the public sector to educate the region's civic and political leaders and the broader public as to regional issues concerning land use and transportation—for example, the recent undertaking by the Northeastern Illinois Planning Commission (NIPC) to develop a regional growth strategy and the development over the last few years of a regional transportation plan by the Chicago Area Transportation Study (CATS), working in close cooperation with NIPC toward the goal of ensuring that transportation and land-use issues are considered on an integrated basis. And there have been joint efforts on the part of public- and private-sector organizations— for example, the Regional Greenways Plan, which is a joint project of NIPC and the Open Lands Project. The principal purpose of that plan is to fill critical gaps in the existing open-space system. Other key organizations serve to facilitate cooperation among political officials at the regional and subregional levels. The most important of these are the Metropolitan Mayors Caucus (which is regionwide), and the DuPage Mayors and Managers Conference, the South Surburban Mayors and Managers Association, and the Northwest Municipal Conference.

The members of the Commercial Club have learned from a number of initiatives that focus on the special opportunities and needs of different parts of the region. For example, Northwest 2001, in the northwest corridor, convenes stakeholders and undertakes initiatives respecting affordable housing, health care, and job training. The East-West Corporate Corridor Association, headquartered in Lombard, focuses on issues of concern to employers in the DuPage County area (for example, issues pertaining to transportation, education, workforce development, and economic development). The South Metropolitan Regional Leadership Center at Governors State University is engaged in a south regional-planning and policy-development process and in an ongoing effort to create a dialogue on the goals of this subregion. Using a computer-based network and a series of grassroots task forces, the Center has implemented policy changes in major areas such as education, environmental quality, land-use planning, diversity, social services, and tax reform.

The American Academy of Arts and Sciences, with the author, is responsible for generating the idea of a study of the American metropolis using metropolitan Chicago as the special focus. This conception evolved into a multiyear project undertaken by the Club in

March 1996. A committee of preeminent experts was formed by the Academy early on to give advice and counsel respecting all aspects of the project leading up to this plan. That committee includes Alan Altshuler, Professor of Urban Policy and Planning at Harvard University's Kennedy School of Government; Richard Briffault, Professor of Law at Columbia University; Anthony Downs, Senior Fellow at the Brookings Institution; Anthony Gómez-Ibañez, Professor, Graduate School of Design at Harvard University; Myron Orfield, Minnesota State Legislator; Henry Richmond, National Growth Management Leadership, Portland, Oregon; David Rusk, Consultant and former Mayor of Albuquerque; and Saskia Sassen, Professor of Sociology at the University of Chicago. Their advice has been invaluable.

We are grateful to the large number of individuals from academia, business, government, and other civic associations who attended many of the committee meetings and helped identify key issues and alternative policy responses. Key advisers included Timothy Bramlet, Anthony Bryk, Julian D'Esposito, Jacques Gordon, J. Alfred Hess, Jr., James Houlihan, Howard Krane, Therese J. McGuire, Robert Miller, Dawn Clark Netsch, Paul Nowicki, Rebecca Riley, Debra Schwartz, Joyce Skoog, Mary Ann Smith, Deborah Stone, Steven Tozer, Mary White, Wim Wiewel, and Paula Wolfe.

The project has been generously funded by the Chicago Community Trust, the Energy Foundation, the John D. and Catherine T. MacArthur Foundation, and the McCormick Tribune Foundation.

Author's Note: The author wishes to express his gratitude to Lawrence Christmas, former Executive Director of NIPC, for his wise counsel at every stage of the project; Laurence O. Booth, a member of the Club and one of Chicago's leading architects, for overseeing the creation and commission of maps and illustrations for the book; Richard L. Thomas, Chairman of the Civic Committee and past Chairman of the Club, for suggesting that the Club assume responsibility for the project; Arnold R. Weber and the six chairs listed in the appendix, for their strong commitment to the project from beginning to end; John Madigan, Chairman of the Club, and Andrew McKenna and George Ranney, Jr., Chairman and President, respectively, of Chicago Metropolis 2020, for their vigorous dedication to the early outreach and implementation phases of the project; and MarySue Barrett, President of the Metropolitan Planning Council, Dea Meyer, Vice President for Policy of the Club's Civic Committee, and Erika Poethig, Associate Project Director, for their outstanding counsel and unwavering support.

INTRODUCTION

THE CHICAGO METROPOLIS 2020 PLAN plan focuses principally on an area of 3,749 square miles of real estate covering six counties and supporting about 7.7 million people and 4.1 million jobs. The six counties are Cook, DuPage, Kane, Lake, McHenry, and Will. This is the area for which the Illinois General Assembly created the Northeastern Illinois Planning Commission (NIPC) in 1957 to conduct comprehensive planning.[1]

The plan is intended to serve as a strategic guide for civic leaders who are working together to prepare metropolitan Chicago for the twenty-first century. Chicago Metropolis 2020 (Metropolis 2020) is the name of the new organization that will facilitate their joint efforts. It is described in the final chapter of this book. The goals of the plan are to enhance the economic vibrancy of the Chicago region and provide the best possible conditions of living for all its residents.[2] The plan has no official status and is not binding on anyone. Rather, it constitutes an open invitation to residents of the region to engage in a public dialogue and to help craft solutions that refine and build on the present document's analyses and recommendations.

The recommendations are driven by a dream of what our region can become in the twenty-first century. We dream of an economically vibrant and environmentally healthy region; one whose concentrated areas of activity enable people of complementary talents to achieve high levels of creativity and productivity; a region where all persons have ready access to jobs, to housing near their jobs, and to good schools and job training; a region in which people are enabled and encouraged to find nourishment in a diversity and complexity of persons, interests, and tastes, and to enjoy an exciting array of cultural, recreational, and intellectual opportunities; and, most important, a region that undergirds strong

> *"O God, grant us a vision of our city, fair as she might be, a city of justice where none shall prey on others, a city of plenty, where vice and poverty shall cease to fester, a city of brotherhood, where all success shall be founded on service, and honour shall be given to nobleness alone, a city of peace, where order shall not rest on force, but on the love of all for the city, the great mother of the common life and weal. Hear though, O Lord, the silent prayer of all our hearts as we each pledge our time and strength and thought to speed the day of her coming beauty and righteousness. Amen."*
>
> WALTER RAUSCHENBUSCH, "PRAYER FOR THE CITY"

neighborhoods, communities, and families so that they are enabled to nurture the intellectual, moral, and social development of children.

The economic and social goals embraced by this dream are closely intertwined. With a strong regional economy, we will have the resources to address the social issues. And as we succeed in putting real teeth and meaning into the ideal of equality of opportunity, we will bring about levels of human productivity and social cohesion that reinforce our economic objectives.

Why should all residents of the region be moved by such a dream? After all, those who dwell in vertically gated communities in downtown Chicago or in spacious homes in the region's many beautiful suburbs have so far been able to live good lives, free of the substantial problems that afflict those suburbs and city neighborhoods that are disadvantaged. And they are well served by a local tax and governance framework and a private transportation system that minimizes their contact with the less pleasant and more risky aspects of urban life.

There are, nevertheless, at least three reasons why all residents of the region should want to pursue such a dream.

First, it is in our near-term self-interest as interdependent residents of one region. This interdependency manifests itself in many ways. The health of every resident depends on the quality of the region's land, air, and water. It is also dependent on the major teaching hospitals that train most of the physicians and surgeons who practice in the region's hospitals. Patients from one part of the region, moreover, often depend on hospitals in another part of the region that specialize in certain surgical procedures.

City residents share a common built environment, and they enjoy suburban music festivals, forest preserves, zoos, and arboretums; and suburban residents are the region's major users of downtown Chicago's chief cultural offerings. A number of universities based in Chicago have suburban campuses that capitalize on the educational resources of the parent institutions.

Enterprises of significant size, which tend to be concentrated in a number of clusters throughout the region, are drawn to the region in order to attract employees with the di-

Chicago's Museum Campus and Lake Shore Drive.

> "The paradox into which one gradually grows, through education and throughout one's life, is that independence is achieved through consenting to interdependence. . . . I believe a state of independence comes when we decide through our intellect and spirit to forge human connections."
>
> A. BARTLETT GIAMATTI,
> FORMER PRESIDENT OF
> YALE UNIVRSITY

versity of skills they require. Thus, for example, 40 percent of workers in both suburban Cook and DuPage Counties live outside those counties. And the Village of Schaumburg, with over 55,000 employees, imports 84 percent of its workers from other communities. Thus, the economic vibrancy of each employment cluster depends on ready access on the part of people throughout the region to goods, services, jobs, and education.

Consider also the economic dependency between central city and suburbs. Suburban residents earn nearly $14 billion a year at jobs in Chicago, almost twice as much as Chicago residents earn in suburban jobs. At the same time, young business executives and professionals who are recruited for jobs in downtown Chicago are drawn to the region by the high quality of residential life both in Chicago's neighborhoods and in the suburbs.

The fate and future of everyone in this region is inherently connected. There is a common interest, a common good, and it cuts across municipal boundaries and binds us all into one metropolitan community. Yet, we have created an increasingly polarized society. The poor live mainly in the central city and inner suburbs, while the more affluent live chiefly in the central core of the city and in the outer suburbs. When a substantial minority of the population is shut out, isolated, and without hope, the economic and social well-being of the whole region is threatened.

Second, more than ever, regions compete against other regions. Our region competes with practically every sizeable metropolis in the nation, and increasingly in the world, based on the quality of life we offer our residents and the quality of the business environment we

TABLE 1   Percentage of Employees Who Work in Their County of Residence

County	Percent
Cook	90.6
DuPage	57.6
Kane	60.1
Lake	63.5
McHenry	50.9
Will	46.2

Source: Census Bureau

hold out to employers. The business corporation, in deciding where to locate a principal office or operation, is increasingly attracted by those regions that offer a large and diverse supply of highly skilled talent; frequent, direct flights to major national and international destinations; large consumer markets; a wide array of technical and professional services; efficient, world-class regional infrastructures and government services; and a strong industrial base of advanced, innovative companies.

Managerial, technical, and professional people, now more footloose than ever before, choose to live in a particular region based on the quality of the firms that are recruiting them; the quality of the region's suburbs and neighborhoods in which they can afford to reside; their proximity to high-quality medical, educational, and cultural institutions; the beauty and excitement of the central city; their access to open space and recreational amenities; and their personal safety.

Moreover, the competitiveness of the entire region will be greatly enhanced by affording the growing population of low-skill workers greater equality of educational opportunity and improved job training.

As we succeed in achieving the dream, we will position our region as one of the world's foremost competitors in the new era of global markets.

Third, and finally, it is the right thing to do. We are more than economic ants busily working on an ever-growing ant hill. Economic growth is not an end in itself and cannot be the only criterion governing our strategies for the region. In this era of unprecedented prosperity, we would be a hollow and nearsighted people indeed if we were to neglect ideals concerning human dignity and equality of opportunity, community and environmental integrity, and the ideals and civilizing purposes of a great metropolitan region. All of us should be driven, first and foremost, by these compelling moral ideals and purposes.

The Burnham Legacy

There is good precedent for placing such importance on the need for a new vision for a new century. Over the first two decades of this past century, the Commercial Club worked with Daniel H. Burnham and Edward H. Bennett to develop a visionary plan for metropolitan Chicago, known as the *Plan of Chicago,* and then to make much of that plan a reality. That plan (the "Burnham Plan"), issued in 1909, is one of the most influential and famous city plans in world history.[3] See appendix A for the remarkable story of the Burnham Plan.

The Burnham Plan, in an economically burgeoning era, focused on the theme of beauty. Jobs were the subject of the Club's effort in 1984,[4] at a time when metropolitan Chicago lagged in the transition from a manufacturing to a service-oriented, "high-tech" economy. The plan set forth here, in the new era of competition among regions, is about the quality of life and equity of opportunity that will be required to assure the economic vitality of the Chicago region.

*The World's Columbian
Exposition of 1893. Plan-
ning for the Exposition was
coordinated by Daniel H.
Burnham.*

This plan calls for a set of public-sector interventions that are quite different from the kinds of public works programs proposed in the Burnham Plan. Our recommendations pertain in large part, but by no means wholly, to the sorts of nonphysical infrastructures that economists and philosophers, from the time of Adam Smith down to the present, have recognized as providing the indispensable background conditions for a dynamic market economy and a good society: for example, a good educational system and a fair and efficient tax system.

As in the case of the Burnham Plan, the new plan speaks not to what is achievable at the moment, but to what is vital for the long term: in short, to direct the development of the region, to paraphrase Daniel Burnham, toward an end that must seem ideal, but is practical. The plan takes stock of the strengths on which the region must build, the new opportunities that it must exploit, and the serious obstacles that must be overcome.

Building on the Region's Strengths

We are in the enviable position of building on a great legacy: the beauty of Chicago's lakefront, unique among all the cities bordering on the Great Lakes; the regional network of rivers, streams, and greenways; the quality and variety of suburban attractions such as the Brookfield Zoo, the Morton Arboretum, the Midewin Tallgrass Prairie Park, the Chicago Botanical Gardens, Ravinia Park, and the major forest preserves; the growth in recent years of suburban institutions devoted to art, music, and the theater; the extensive mass-transit infrastructure that we still enjoy; the importance of the region as the nation's single most important airline and railway hub; the excellence of the region's universities and medical institutions; the economic diversity and strength of the city and the several regional centers; the cultural vitality and architectural splendors of downtown Chicago, and the pedestrian liveliness of its streets; the enduring strength and richness of the region's ethnic neighborhoods; and the strong tradition of the region's civic associations in cooperating with political leaders to advance the common interests of all parts of the region.

One of the things that distinguishes the region from most other large metropolitan areas and accounts for many of its unique strengths is the major role played by the public sector in shaping the physical environment of downtown Chicago and the lakefront, much or most of it in pursuance of the Burnham Plan. It is naive to think that the private market, by itself, could have created a center of such beauty and vibrancy. In recent years, we have experienced something of a Burnham-like renaissance of interest in and near the lakefront: a newly transformed Navy Pier; the re-routing of Lake Shore Drive to create a campus for the three museums located on the near south side (the Field Museum of Natural History, the Shedd Aquarium, and the Adler Planetarium);[5] the recent completion of a beautiful lighted walkway on the north side of the Chicago River, stretching from Michigan Avenue

> *"Make no little plans. They have no magic to stir men's blood and probably themselves will not be realized. Make big plans; aim high in hope and work, remembering that a noble, logical diagram once recorded will never die, but long after we are gone will be a living thing, asserting itself with ever-growing insistency. Remember that our sons and grandsons are going to do things that would stagger us."*
>
> DANIEL BURNHAM

for several blocks to the east; the new site for the Museum of Contemporary Art on the near north side; a breathtaking transformation and expansion of the Chicago Symphony's concert hall and related facilities; and most recently, Mayor Daley's unveiling of a $150 million "Lakefront Millennium Project," intended to enhance park, recreation, cultural, and transportation facilities along Chicago's lakefront in the area of Grant Park.

The other development in the core area of Chicago over the last decade has been the explosion in residential development, all within a few miles of the city center. Some are newly constructed units on formerly vacant railroad yards (for example, Dearborn Park, on thirty-one acres immediately south of the Loop), or on sites where older residential or commercial buildings were torn down. Many more of the new residential units have been created by converting former office and warehouse buildings and by rehabilitating old, deteriorated residential buildings.

In some of Chicago's neighborhoods that have suffered the greatest economic deterioration, job loss, and depopulation over the last few decades—neighborhoods with high rates of crime and drug trafficking—there are examples of rejuvenation: for example, North Kenwood/Oakland and Woodlawn on the south side, North Lawndale on the west side, and Logan Square on the near northwest side. The plan places a high priority on further strengthening the community development efforts that produced much of this rejuvenation of residential and retail life.

In the suburbs, there is evidence of sensible growth policies that encourage mixed-use developments near transit and/or employment centers (for example, Arlington Heights and Naperville) and the rehabilitation of historic downtown districts (for example, Downers Grove, Lake Forest, Lockport, and Wheaton). The plan's land-use and housing policy recommendations will greatly facilitate the spread of these policies.

Finally the region's caregiving organizations, foundations, and faith-based associations are central to the region's vitality. Many of the strategies recommended in this plan are geared to the region's unique partnerships among public, private, and nonprofit sectors.

Exploiting the New Possibilities of Life in the Metropolis

Cities have always existed and flourished because proximity is a prerequisite to specialization of labor and to the sustenance of a high level of civilization. But the conditions and reasons for proximity have changed greatly. For most of the last two hundred years, the industrial revolution was the great urbanizing force in this country. Until well into the twentieth century, manufacturing and packing plants had to be located near ports and freight rail terminals in the center city, where employees were forced to work in the crowded core. This created a terrible tension between the city as economic engine and the city as center of culture, intellectual excitement, beauty, and community. Then, beginning in the prosperous 1920s, and resuming and continuing throughout the sustained period of prosperity following World War II, metropolitan regions in the United States underwent a process, unprecedented in scale, of deconcentration—decentralizing both economic activity and residential life. The factors that brought about this process are recounted in appendix B.

Does this mean that physical proximity no longer matters? Not at all. Today, information technologies have made large metropolitan areas with vital regional centers the favored location for knowledge-based industries by reason of their heavy dependence on "smart" buildings wired with high-speed communications lines and other digital amenities and their need for ready access to skilled workers, suppliers, and research universities. As Michael Porter, professor at Harvard University, has recently observed, "Cities are aligned with the nature of modern competition, with its emphasis on fluidity, information flow, and innovation. Cities are centers of knowledge and expertise, the most precious assets in the global economy."[6]

More than ever before, talented professionals and entrepreneurs will be attracted by the region's facilities for easy networking, for its turbulence, and for its openness to new ideas. They will be drawn by the cultural richness and physical beauty of the region. And dual-career couples will be attracted by the amenities and services located in the region's high-density centers near home or work, allowing them to fulfill their household responsibilities in the most efficient manner.

For the first time since the birth of the industrial revolution, we can think and dream about cities as the philosophers of old once did. We can live and work in metropolitan areas that are healthful and neighborly and civilized. No longer must we deal with some basic conflict between the economic and social purposes of cities. We can seize the moment and begin to build transportation and communication systems and public-policy frameworks that reinforce the advantages of proximity in a multicentered metropolis.

Overcoming the Obstacles

These are exciting possibilities, but three major obstacles threaten the goals of the plan. The first concerns the need to ensure that all the region's children have access to good health care and a high-quality education from infancy to age eighteen and that all the region's adults have access to high-quality workforce development programs that will enable them to develop their skills to the fullest. The new international economic order is placing ever greater premiums on educated skills. This is an exciting development, provided we take seriously the ideal of equal opportunity.

The second obstacle is posed by the spatial transformation of the metropolis. A totally new urban form has emerged across America: a dispersed and stratified agglomeration of people that is neither village nor city. The old central city was hollowed out as middle- and upper-income households prospered and were able to realize their dream of each owning a couple of motor vehicles and living in a detached single-family home in a safe and pleasant suburb with neighbors of similar socioeconomic characteristics. Employers followed along, and sophisticated providers of goods and services created new "edge" cities where they could best cater to their segmented markets. The technological, market, and demographic forces that accounted for these new spatial patterns showed no signs of abating until the 1990s.

The benefits to the majority have been accompanied by serious costs, borne mostly by those living in distressed areas of the central city and in the worse-off suburbs. Yet, increasingly, many of the costs are being felt by the entire metropolitan region. The key problem is the bias in our governance and tax framework that often discourages localities from acting in the regional interest. This bias is exacerbated by the sheer number of autonomous governmental units in the region and the lack of a coordinating mechanism with significant authority to address regional issues.

In part, decisions as to urban form should be collective and deliberated on a metropolitan scale, rather than being wholly the inadvertent product of private-market and local zoning decisions within a flawed policy framework.

The third obstacle is posed by the high levels of concentrated poverty and racial and social segregation in our region. It is true that the size of the underclass seems to be shrinking. For example, as African Americans have succeeded in their struggle to achieve equal liberties and opportunities, they have made great progress in the workplace. Yet, the residential isolation of poor minorities has actually worsened in the last two decades.

Four out of five poor whites live in mixed-income neighborhoods within the region, but only one in five poor blacks do. The hyperconcentration of the minority poor, combined with the technological transformation of the economic order, has created levels of joblessness, social isolation, and family and community dysfunction that have severely handicapped their opportunity for a better life.

All of these challenges and opportunities cry out for the kind of plan that follows—a plan in which the region can shape and redirect its actions during the coming decades.

PART ONE
GOALS, CHALLENGES, AND
GUIDING PRINCIPLES

The Six Committees and the Organization of the Plan

The plan is based on the work of six committees, composed of members of the Commercial Club, established in the fall of 1996. Each committee was assigned responsibility for one of the following areas: economic development, education, governance, land use and housing, taxation, and transportation. The chairs and vice chairs of these six committees and the members of the steering committee are listed in appendix C.

During the first year of the project, the six committees held numerous meetings. More than 200 members of the Club were engaged in these meetings, working with outside experts. In addition, four meetings of the full membership were held during the first year to consider key issues and react to committee reports. Based on those reports and the members' comments, the author drafted chapters which were considered by all the members in a series of meetings held during the second year. Numerous other meetings were held with local and regional policymakers and stakeholders, including a three-day retreat in May 1998, where more than 120 regional leaders and their spouses gathered to review and comment on an overview of the draft of the plan. Throughout this interactive process, the chapters were periodically revised by the author in consultation with the six committees. The final document was unanimously approved by the members at a meeting held on November 19, 1998.

The plan is divided into two parts: goals, challenges, and guiding principles; and recommendations. A special final chapter, "Outreach and Implementation," describes Metropolis 2020, the organization that will be responsible for communicating the plan, prioritizing the recommendations, developing definitive proposals that have widespread support, and working toward the goals of the plan.

For the most part, the achievement of the plan's goals for the region is up to individuals, families, neighborhoods, and business enterprises in the free and vigorous pursuit of their private interests. But there are three basic supporting roles that government must perform. First, government must provide the kinds of background conditions and public services (for example, physical infrastructure systems and their maintenance, educational systems, police and fire protection, and related tax and governance arrangements) that enable individuals, groups, and enterprises to flourish.

Second, state government should impose rules of the game to ensure that homebuilders operate in a free-market system in meeting the demand for housing throughout the region and to discourage municipalities from using their zoning and other laws to undermine such a market.

Third, state government must provide the kinds of policy frameworks and public services that facilitate the collective efforts of citizens to focus on the common good (for example, the environment) and that enable and encourage the least advantaged citizens to better their condition.

In performing these roles, government should exhaust the possibilities of harnessing the energy of the private sector, whether through marketlike incentives, or subcontracting, or privatization, so that individuals and enterprises are strongly motivated to correlate the pursuit of their private interests with the larger public good, so that the costs of government are minimized, and so that the efficiencies of the private sector are fully exploited.

No functions should be performed by government that can better be performed in the private sector; and no functions should be carried out by federal, state, or regional government if those functions can be performed well by local government. In brief, then, these are the principles that have guided the members of the Commercial Club in addressing the challenges presented in part 1.

PUBLIC EDUCATION AND CHILD CARE

Nothing affecting the region's economic vitality in the next century will be as important as the quality of health care, nurture, and education provided to the region's children. This chapter focuses on those challenges. First, there must be continuous improvement in all the region's public schools for students in grades K through 12 and radical improvement in the educational effectiveness of its lowest performing schools. The second challenge is to design and implement a system that gives every child, no matter how poor, access to good health care. Third is the need for care and programs for infants and preschool children, especially those in low-income families.

Public Education

The goal is to ensure that all the region's children have equal access to a high-quality education from infancy to age eighteen. There are three principal reasons why this goal has not been achieved. First, educational funding is heavily dependent on local property taxes, and some property-rich districts spend nearly four times as much per student as the poorest districts, creating large differences in teacher salaries and physical facilities and class size. The plan proposes reforms in the property tax system to bring about a more equitable means of funding public education.

The second reason is the failure, particularly in Chicago but also in many suburbs, to properly educate and train well-qualified persons as principals and teachers in sufficient

> *"That political economy which busies itself about capital and labor, supply and demand, interest and rents, favorable balances of trade, but leaves out of account the element of a widespread mental development, is nought but stupendous folly."*
>
> ⬌
>
> HORACE MANN

numbers to make a difference, to introduce ongoing mechanisms for professional development and incentives for superior performance, and to establish effective systems of governance that combine high levels of accountability and professionalism. There has been tangible progress in the City of Chicago in addressing this second set of problems, but much remains to be done. The plan proposes far-reaching reforms to bring about a much more results-oriented approach to school performance. Third, most of the lowest performing schools are located in severely disadvantaged neighborhoods. Thus, achieving the goal of equality of educational opportunity entails long-term strategies aimed at increasing economic and social opportunities for poor minorities.

BACKGROUND

More than 1.2 million students are currently enrolled in primary and secondary public schools throughout the region. In 1996–97, the public-school population in the six-county area was as follows: the City of Chicago, 421,300; suburban Cook County, 356,400; the collar counties, 453,300. About 166,000 children (three-fourths of them in Chicago) attended parochial schools in the region in that school year, and perhaps another 10,000 attended other private schools. In 1990, nonwhites accounted for about 40 percent of the elementary-school population in the region, and they are expected to account for 57 percent by the year 2020. The most dramatic growth will be in the Hispanic student population, which is expected to increase by 272,000, or 120 percent, between 1990 and 2020. These regional figures mask the fact that in Chicago 89 percent of the student population is nonwhite.

The responsibility of the region's public systems of elementary and high schools, ideally, is to equip students with the basic knowledge, skills, and attributes that will enable them to develop good work skills and live richly satisfying lives; that will prepare a substantial portion of them for some form of higher education; and that will prepare all of them to be good citizens and neighbors, nurturing parents, and individuals capable of making positive contributions to their communities.

A century and a half ago, Horace Mann, the great evangelist for the common school and secretary of education in Massachusetts for twelve years, articulated the strong connection between education and economic prosperity. In response to hardheaded businessmen of his time, who doubted the value of universal education, Mann conducted extensive investigations showing the vast difference in productive capacity between educated and uneducated workers. He concluded that "the aim of industry is served, and the wealth of the country is augmented, in proportion to the diffusion of knowledge."[1]

In Mann's time, the country was undergoing a fundamental change from an agrarian to an industrial economy, and the need for new kinds of educated work skills had become

> *"You in your classrooms have more of an opportunity to change the moral landscape of our little universe than the doctor does in the hospital, than the lawyer does in the court, than the reporter does on the newspaper, than the engineer does in the field."*
>
> ━━━
>
> VIVIAN PALEY'S
> VALEDICTORY MESSAGE TO
> SCHOOLTEACHERS

acute. In a parallel way, we are currently moving from an industrial economy to one that is much more knowledge based. Thus, his words are as timely now as they were in the 1830s when he wrote them. In today's global marketplace, the competitive advantage of our region depends more than ever on the skills and capabilities of our workers in comparison with those of workers in other important economic regions of the world. Given America's increasing outsourcing of low-skill work to other countries and the use of new technologies that reduce the need for low-skill labor in this country, we have a choice. We can increase the proportion of high-wage jobs in the region's workforce and enhance its attractiveness to prospective employers by building a public school system geared to producing graduates who qualify for such jobs. Or, in the alternative, we can continue turning out far too many young adults who are ill-equipped to earn a living wage, thereby undermining the productivity of the entire region and its appeal to prospective employers and residents.

SIZING UP THE PROBLEM

How do the region's schools measure up? And compared to what? Student test scores, admittedly an imperfect form of measurement, portray a dismal picture. In a study of math and science skills among half a million thirteen-year-olds from forty-one nations, U.S. students ranked twenty-eighth in mathematics and seventeenth in science. Singapore scored first in both subjects, followed, in mathematics, by South Korea, Japan, and Hong Kong.[2]

Averages do not convey the full story. The Chicago metropolitan region is home to suburban schools whose students' scores in math and science are world-class. And six of the ten top elementary schools in Illinois in terms of Illinois Goals Assessment Program (IGAP) reading and math scores in a recent year were in Chicago. But a very large number of schools were at the opposite extreme. In the fall of 1998, the Illinois State Board of Education (ISBE) placed 60 schools throughout the region on an academic early warning list. All except two of these schools were located in the City of Chicago. In the same year, the Chicago Public School System had placed 35 of the city's 74 high schools and 23 of its 483 elementary schools on probation, primarily on the basis of low test scores.

By any reasonable measure, more than half of the region's schools can be categorized as "low-performing." Not surprisingly, the great majority of them are located in the region's poorest communities. In addition to poverty and unemployment, these places are also likely to have a high incidence of drug use and gang and criminal activity, all of which pose additional obstacles in the way of educational achievement.

There are other ways, besides test scores, of sizing up the educational effectiveness of the public schools. For example, one can look at dropout rates, attendance, teacher turnover, parent surveys, employer surveys, and whether there's been a growing need for the private sector to provide remedial education and job training programs that teach basic elementary and high school level skills. Most of these other indicators reinforce the need to focus on the same schools that we have identified using the criterion of test scores.

PROGRESS IN CHICAGO

Despite this gloomy snapshot, the Chicago school system, which includes most of the region's low-performing schools serving the bottom tier of household income, has made remarkable progress over the past decade. One of the reasons is a series of legislative reforms by the State of Illinois, which has ultimate responsibility under the 1970 Constitution to provide "for an efficient system of high quality public educational institutions and services." These reforms were stimulated in large measure by vigorous and sustained advocacy on the part of a wide array of business and civic leaders, as well as concentrated efforts by parents, community-based groups, and education-related organizations throughout the state.

The 1988 reforms were aimed at creating a base of local leadership that would sustain a serious focus on school improvement. These reforms have gone a long way in improving community relations, parent involvement, school safety, and, in many cases, particularly at the elementary school level, academic performance.

The 1995 and 1997 reforms conferred on the mayor of Chicago direct responsibility for the school system, with power to appoint the members of the new Reform Board and certain of the top officers; to channel the influence of the system's unions in more constructive ways; and to greatly simplify the system's finances. Most of the local decision-making powers created by the 1988 reforms were left in place, but the central system was given new authority to engage underperforming schools.

In the last few years, Mayor Daley has instituted numerous reforms that have raised the level of accountability among students, teachers, and principals and that have improved the physical facilities of the system. Nevertheless, most of Chicago's schools, particularly the high schools, are still operating below a minimally acceptable level of performance.[3]

THE 1997 LEGISLATIVE REFORMS

In late 1997, the state legislature amended a number of education acts. Reforms that year established a statewide "foundation," or minimum, level of funding of $4,225 per student in the first year (1998–99), to increase by $100 in each of the two succeeding years. In addition, the law provided for poverty grants to districts based on concentrations of poverty, initially from $800 to $1,900 per pupil, depending on the degree of concentration. The law also provided $1.4 billion in critically needed funds to repair the state's crumbling schools and to build new facilities.

Of managerial reforms provisions, the most significant in terms of improving student achievement were those pertaining to the Initial Teaching Certificate and the first Standard Teaching Certificate. They enable the ISBE to upgrade the quality of the teaching staff by screening out both unqualified applicants for the initial certificate and poorly performing teachers who apply for the standard certificate. To do so, the ISBE will need to depart sharply from its deeply entrenched practices of the past several decades. Moreover, it will remain extraordinarily difficult to terminate a bad teacher after he or she once receives a Standard Teaching Certificate, given the ease of renewal and the bureaucratic roadblocks with which a principal must contend in the course of the termination process.

The other promising provision was the "Alternative Route to Teacher Certification" program. This program, if properly designed and implemented, could provide the means for significantly increasing the number of well-qualified teachers by attracting bright, highly motivated people who have worked for a period of time in other endeavors and who would like to become teachers, provided they are not frustrated at the outset by inappropriate red tape and excessive emphasis on education methodology.[4]

THE ILLINOIS STATE BOARD OF EDUCATION

All public primary and secondary schools in the state are under the oversight of the ISBE. The ISBE was created by the State Constitution, which provides that the Board "may establish goals, determine policies, provide for planning and evaluating education programs and recommend financing." But it is the School Code of 1961, as amended,[5] which sets out the detailed powers and responsibilities of the Board and of each school district board. That code, much like the Internal Revenue Code of the United States, currently runs to well over one thousand pages. This is in sharp contrast to the much briefer set of laws covering higher education in Illinois.

Whereas the boards of trustees of the state's public colleges and universities are given broad discretion in managing the affairs of their respective institutions, the School Code lays down, according to a recent ISBE task force, a "complicated array of certificates and endorsements through a cumbersome structure of administrative approvals and variations on these approvals." For decades the Board has required its approval of all teacher preparation programs at all Illinois institutions of higher education, "in a process that is time consuming for each institution, but which rarely if ever [results in an instance of disapproval]." These approved teaching programs are designed "without substantial involvement of practicing teachers." While forty-three states require professional development for renewal of standard teaching certificates, the Board has never undertaken any such effort, and aside from a "course counting approach," the only real requirement for certificate renewal is the payment of a few dollars in annual fees. Finally, a bureaucratic culture of long standing has made it next to impossible to terminate bad teachers; and the Code, by failing to specify the areas that should be nonnegotiable (such as flexible work rules), permits school districts and unions to enter into contracts that undermine the possibilities of educational excellence.[6]

Notwithstanding many hopeful signs and sincere efforts by past state superintendents to transform the agency, the question is whether any state superintendent, no matter how visionary and forceful, can overcome the feudalism of a bureaucratic staff. Many of the personnel have been in place for decades and owe their job security to legislative members, on both sides of the aisle, with whom they stay in close communication.

THE HEART OF THE MATTER

Much remains to be done, but the educational reforms of the last ten years have laid the beginnings of a foundation for addressing the challenges before us:

➤ To attract, train, retain, and motivate a critical mass of teachers who become so adept at their profession, so competent in the subjects they teach, and so effective in moti-

vating their students, that many or most of the students become engaged in the learning process to their full capacities, even those who must overcome significant obstacles to achievement by reason of family and neighborhood circumstances.

► To enable an increasingly diverse immigrant student population to participate fully in the social and economic mainstream of America.

► To tend more carefully to the special needs of disabled children.

► To upgrade the institutions that educate the region's new teachers so that they attract better qualified students and so that their graduates are better prepared to teach.

► To create a mutual support system among teachers within each school so that the more able, experienced teachers are enabled and expected to coach and mentor younger teachers.

► To enable this same mutual support system to identify those among their peers who have proved incapable of meeting the demanding standards of the profession and who must be terminated to make room for more talented, more dedicated persons, and to institute mechanisms for pruning out of the system those teachers so identified for termination and providing them with counseling.

► To improve the core curricula across all grades, using the best available teaching materials.

> ► To create a sense of community within each school so that it becomes a place for education in justice and citizenship.

> ► And to meet the dire need for programs and care for preschool children—especially those children who must have nurture outside the home if they are to have any realistic chance of succeeding in elementary school and beyond.[7]

To meet these challenges, we must begin by understanding the bureaucratic mind-set that was built up over many decades and that has made school reform very much of an uphill battle.

A number of experts in education have identified the core problem posed by the traditional bureaucracy as being that of a deeply entrenched "input regulation" approach.[8] This traditional approach, followed in the State of Illinois and across much of the nation, is highly centralized, and it focuses on regulating various dimensions of school life: teacher certification, minimum hours of daily instruction and number of days in the school year, graduation requirements in terms of the number of specific courses passed, and so forth. "The assumption behind this approach," says G. Alfred Hess, Jr., "is that if every school in the state utilizes minimally acceptable inputs, acceptable student learning will result and differences in student achievement will reflect either the latent talent of the students or the effort they are willing to put forward."[9]

By contrast, the performance-based approach is the competitive market model. In the business world, the managers of enterprises are held accountable on the basis of results. They have a free hand, within legal and ethical constraints, in determining how to achieve good results for their stockholders. The CEO of a large corporation with many decentralized, highly autonomous operating units may spend 80 percent of his or her time monitoring the performance of the 10 percent of the units that are underperforming, pressing for improvement, and ultimately replacing management if all else fails. The bureaucratic model may formally provide for performance-based accountability, but the standards are usually subject to manipulation and are notoriously difficult to implement in complex, nonmarket organizations.

The competitive model implies a measure of school choice. In the world of business, some of our largest, most bureaucratic corporations have been restructured and reenergized as a result of the new competition they have had to face from abroad. Within the world of education, competition among a large number of private and public universities has been effective in creating lasting incentives for institutions to improve services for all segments of the population. This competition has made the United States the world leader in providing higher education. Another example, which involves both a private-sector entity and a large bureaucracy, is that of Federal Express. While public education is far more complex than delivering packages, there may be an instructive analogy here: the introduction of an alternative carrier has had significant impact on both the improvement and expansion of postal delivery in this country.

The performance-based (results-oriented) approach, as applied to education, does not mean a rugged individualistic culture. The goal is to graduate students who have learned

their subjects well and who have developed their capacities for ethical citizenship. To these ends, collegiality and cooperation among the teachers and a sense of community among students and faculty are crucial.

The recommendations in chapter 6 are geared to effecting the kinds of governance and organizational changes that will accelerate the move from the traditional approach to a much more professional and performance-based approach. We are mindful of the fact that such facilitating changes are not sufficient in and of themselves. According to Richard Elmore, "The central problem of performance-based accountability is the hardest part: learning how to reach large numbers of teachers in their classrooms, as they engage in the daily work of teaching, in ways that are designed to provide them with the knowledge they require to teach differently and to produce different results for students."[10] But if schools are to work toward the kind of professionalism and teacher development that a performance-based system entails, they must have an organizational environment that is conducive to, not obstructive of, that end.

In truth, our nation's educational policymakers, practitioners, and researchers are just beginning to explore how to bring about this fundamental transformation. It is clear, however, that demands for accountability, to be effective, must be accompanied by the confer-

> "Can we motivate children born into poor environments to look at life and school with an expectation of success? The task is a difficult one, but we can learn how to ensure good self-esteem in all our children and encourage them to begin life motivated to succeed and with the belief that they can succeed."
>
> ⟷
>
> IRVING HARRIS,
> *CHILDREN IN JEOPARDY*

ring of power, authority, and resources on those we intend to hold responsible for results. Those persons, above all others, are the school principals, and in order for them to succeed in an environment in which they are held accountable for student performance, they must have the requisite management and leadership skills to allocate resources in optimal ways, to identify and attract good teachers, to identify and terminate bad teachers, and to foster a high degree of professionalism and team play.

Child Care

This section addresses the needs of low- and middle-income working parents for quality, affordable child care. Quality care enables infants and young children to become emotionally secure, socially competent, and intellectually capable. Children who receive inadequate or barely adequate care are more likely to feel insecure with a teacher, to distrust other children, and to face rejection by other children. All these factors are powerful predictors of future school performance.

The single most important factor driving the demand for institutionalized forms of child care in this country is the increasing participation of women from all income levels in the workforce. Whereas only 17 percent of mothers of one-year-olds worked full-time or part-time in 1965, fully 53 percent were in the labor force in 1991. In 1995, 60 percent of women with children under age six worked, and 75 percent of women with children ages six to seventeen worked. Eight out of ten employed mothers with children under six are likely to use some form of nonparental child-care arrangement. Based on 1993 data, child-care centers represent 30 percent of the primary child-care arrangement, followed by non-relative family child care (21 percent), grandparents (17 percent), father (16 percent), other relatives (9 percent), and mother (6 percent).

EDUCATING AND CARING FOR PRESCHOOL CHILDREN

The quality and affordability of preschool care and education is a regional issue. First, the effectiveness of the region's public-education system and its workforce development programs depends heavily on the quality of care and nurture that preschool children receive, either at home or in an institutionalized setting. It is estimated that 35 percent of children who show up in kindergarten classrooms are not ready to learn.

Second, the productivity of low- and middle-income working parents of preschool children, not to mention the quality of their lives, is seriously affected when they are under financial and psychological stress because their children are enrolled at high cost in facilities of poor quality.

Both low-income and middle-income parents are adversely affected by: (1) the cost of child care, which can make employment less attractive; (2) the quality of the child-care providers; and (3) the availability of child care, especially near or in the family home, and on evenings and weekends. The cost of child care is usually prohibitive for those who need to or are required to work by federal law. In 1995, a single mother earning the minimum wage brought home only $8,840. To procure a formal child-care arrangement, she would have to spend 38 percent of that income. The majority of the women who will be required to move from welfare to work have more than one child, doubling and sometimes tripling the cost of child care. One-third of poor mothers are not in the labor force because of child-care problems.

The other key problem is the paucity of qualified child-care professionals. The turnover rates among child-care providers exceeds 40 percent annually. Low wages, poor benefits, and limited professional esteem are the major barriers to attracting qualified people to the field of early childhood development. Yet, teaching preschool children may require more skill and education than teaching at the elementary school level. A revolving door of teachers is not very reassuring to children or very healthy for their social development. Insecure children may grow up to be insecure adults, unable to thrive in a school or work environment.

FINANCING CHILD CARE

State of Illinois. In the fiscal year ending in 1999, the State of Illinois will have spent $391.5 million on child care, up from $280.6 million in 1996. This increase, combined with stricter eligibility and co-pay requirements, has enabled the state to substantially reduce the waiting list for subsidized care and provide child-care assistance for all families below 50 percent of the state median income.

Private employers. In the past five years, major corporations have invested more than $350 million nationally (perhaps as much as $25 million in our region) in child-care initiatives. Most of these funds have been targeted to start new child-care centers, recruit new family child-care homes, and improve the quality of child care. Less frequently, employers have established dependent-care assistance plans that help reduce the cost of child care by reducing employee tax burdens or providing more flexible working arrangements. Few employers actually subsidize the weekly cost of child care for their employees.

It is in the long-term interests of private employers to provide child-care assistance to employees. When a parent is worried about the quality of their child-care arrangement, they are more distracted and less focused. Also, child-care programs can be an effective recruiting tool. More generally, the quality of the future workforce depends as much on the quality of early childhood care as on the quality of public-school education.

THE ACCREDITATION AND LICENSING SYSTEM

As of October 1999, 323 of Illinois' child-care centers had been accredited by the National Association for the Education of Young Children (NAEYC), based on stringent quality standards. These centers meet the highest standards of care and early education, but unfortunately they represent only a small fraction of the licensed centers in the region. In Cook County alone, the Department of Child and Family Services has licensed 1,196 daycare centers and another 2,449 daycare homes (each typically caring for three to twelve children). Licensing standards, set at the state level, are primarily based on health and safety criteria that are geared to minimal levels of custodial care, not to quality of educational nurture.

HEALTH CARE FOR UNINSURED POOR CHILDREN

There are 300,000 children in the State of Illinois who are uninsured, and most of them live in families below twice the level of the federal poverty line. The poor are disproportionately affected by diseases that are largely preventable, but costly if left untreated, such as diabetes, hypertension, asthma, and the problems associated with low-birth-weight babies. There is, of course, a close link between children's health and their educability and their potential to become vital members of the community. Equality of opportunity is a hollow ideal where basic health care is not delivered. We must redesign the delivery system if we are to moderate existing inequities and narrow the gap between poorer and wealthier communities.

TRANSPORTATION

*T*he region's future depends on a personal transportation system that enables the region's residents, across the spectrums of age and income, to move about in ways that are safe, convenient, and comfortable. They should be able to view clear skies, breathe clean air, and enjoy pleasant environments for walking and bicycling. They should have access to a wide range of housing choices in locations that enable them to reduce the number and length of their daily trips. The various modes of transportation in the region should be complementary, encouraging people to switch easily from one mode to another, utilizing fully the advantages of all modes. Public transit must be safe and its use encouraged by land-use policies that promote higher-density, mixed-use developments around important rail and transit stations.

Chicago has long been at the crossroads of America, and in the new era of global markets, it is more important than ever to provide ease of intermodal connection among all modes of freight transportation and to anticipate and provide for the region's growing demand for air service.

This chapter is divided into three sections: personal mobility within the region; freight transportation to, from, and within the region; and air and rail transport of people to and from the region.

Personal Mobility within the Region

Private motor vehicle use now accounts for more than 90 percent of all personal surface travel in this region. In 1990, 68 percent of all commuting trips in the region were made in solo-driven vehicles, up from 58 percent in 1980.

The continued dispersion of jobs away from the center city will tend to intensify our automobile dependency. The Northeastern Illinois Planning Commission (NIPC) projects the addition of 1.8 million people and 1.4 million jobs between now and 2020 and predicts that this growth will take place largely outside the Chicago city limits, as shown in table 2.

TABLE 2   Regional Job Growth to the Year 2020

Subregion	*1990 Jobs*	*Growth to 2020*	*Total 2020 Jobs*	*% Growth*
City of Chicago	1,480,000	260,000	1,740,000	18
Suburban Cook County	1,290,000	480,000	1,770,000	37
DuPage County	530,000	285,000	815,000	54
Other Counties	545,000	410,000	955,000	75

Source: NIPC

MOTOR VEHICLE TRANSPORTATION

The motor vehicle will remain the dominant form of personal transportation for the foreseeable future. Its extensive use is made possible by the region's current network of more than 54,000 lane miles of roads,[1] which are used for both personal vehicle trips and the hauling of goods by truck, and which accommodate approximately 16 million vehicle trips per day. Between 1985 and 1995, vehicle miles of travel in the region increased by almost 40 percent, but the number of lane miles increased by only 5 percent. The largest increase was in DuPage and McHenry Counties, where vehicle travel jumped 60 percent.

The motor vehicle has enriched our lives in countless ways. It has provided the easy connectivity that enables modern, highly interdependent, urban societies to thrive. It has enabled workers to choose employers rather than accept whatever employment opportunities are within walking or transit distance of their homes. The personal truck allowed craftspeople and artisans to become independent contractors and enter the middle class. The car has greatly extended our range of choice as to where to live, work, shop, and play. No other form of transport can compete with the private motor vehicle in terms of door-to-door mobility, freedom to time one's arrivals and exits, protection from inclement weather, and comfort, security, and privacy while in transit.

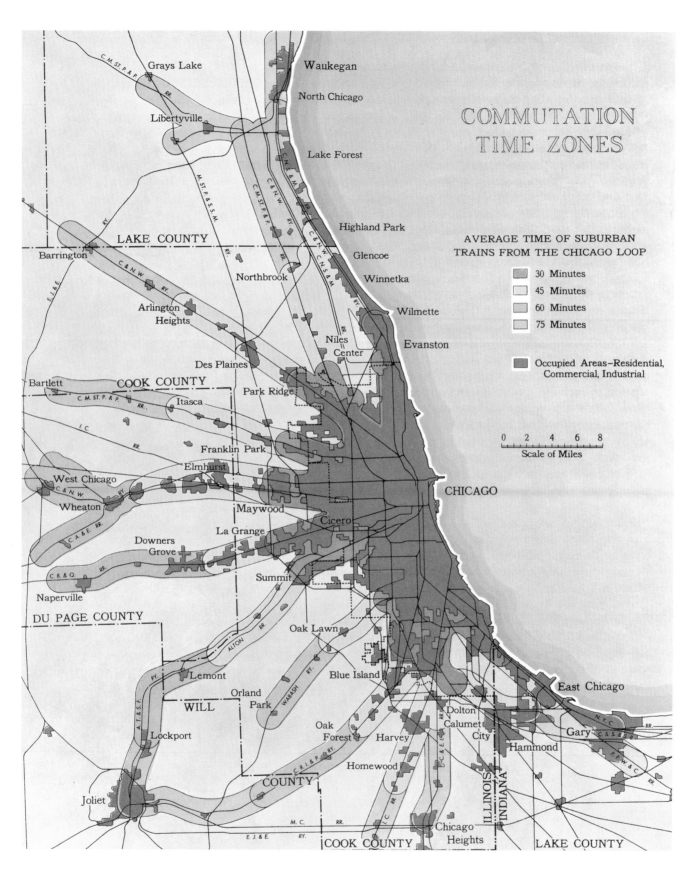

COMMUTATION
TIME ZONES

AVERAGE TIME OF SUBURBAN
TRAINS FROM THE CHICAGO LOOP

30 Minutes
45 Minutes
60 Minutes
75 Minutes

Occupied Areas—Residential,
Commercial, Industrial

0   2   4   6   8
Scale of Miles

Grays Lake
Waukegan
North Chicago
Libertyville
Lake Forest
LAKE COUNTY
Barrington
Highland Park
Glencoe
Northbrook
Winnetka
Arlington
Heights
Wilmette
Niles
Center
Evanston
Des Plaines
Bartlett
COOK COUNTY
Park Ridge
Itasca
Franklin Park
Elmhurst
West Chicago
Wheaton
Maywood
Cicero
CHICAGO
La Grange
Downers
Grove
Naperville
Summit
DU PAGE COUNTY
Oak Lawn
Lemont
Blue Island
Orland
Park
East Chicago
WILL
Lockport
Oak
Forest
Dolton
Calumet
City
Harvey
Gary
Hammond
Homewood
COUNTY
Chicago
Heights
COOK COUNTY
ILLINOIS
INDIANA
LAKE COUNTY

A look at commuting times in the year 1956. (Drawing by Miles Sater)

Yet, over-reliance on this one form of personal mobility in a metropolitan setting has posed serious problems. For one thing, 35 percent of households in the City of Chicago do not own a motor vehicle. This compares with 3 to 8 percent in the collar counties of the region. For those who do not have access to a vehicle, or are too young, too old, or too infirm to drive, the paucity of mobility alternatives severely limits their opportunities for education and employment and their ability to share in other essential, everyday activities. The problem has been exacerbated as more employers have moved to the suburbs where access to jobs requires car mobility.

Second, the private motor vehicle is not designed to gather masses of people from low-density areas of the region and transport them to high-density centers. And these core areas cannot accommodate the many thousands of parked vehicles without detracting from the compactness and pedestrian liveliness of such areas.

Third, traffic congestion continues to worsen throughout the region. The Chicago region has the second largest number of workers (10.7 percent) in the nation with average commute times of at least sixty minutes each way. The national average for regions with populations of more than one million is 7.5 percent.

While commuting times, on average, have not increased appreciably over the last two decades, it is estimated that vehicle travel on congested roads will increase almost twice as much (by 60 percent) as total vehicle travel, assuming that only previously committed improvements to the road and transit systems are made.

A fourth problem, arising out of the region's heavy reliance on the motor vehicle, is that of air pollution. The Chicago area is the nation's second most serious nonattainment region in terms of the number of days each year in which the area fails to meet National Ambient Air Quality Standards for ozone. Motor vehicles account for about one-third of this problem. Despite the billions of dollars that have been spent on revolutionary new vehicle and fuel technologies over the last two or three decades, the problem has not been solved because (1) about half of all new vehicles sold are light trucks, vans, and recreational vehicles, which are held to far less stringent fuel efficiency and emissions standards than are cars; (2) the increasing amount of stop-and-start, low-speed driving, due to congestion, as well as the high level (50 percent) of urban vehicle trips of less than five miles, pollutes the air far out of proportion to the number of miles driven; and (3) commuters going to work in metropolitan business centers in the United States in their own motor vehicles directly pay for only about 25 percent of the total costs of their transport. The other 75 percent is typically borne by their employers (for example, in providing "free" parking), by other users (in increased congestion, reduced safety, etc.), by fellow workers or residents (in air or noise pollution, etc.), and by governments (passed on to taxpayers of one generation or the next in ways that bear no relationship to motor vehicle use).

When a product as central to American life as the automobile remains underpriced for several decades, that product tends to be used more than it otherwise would be. Thus, we now drive twice as many miles as in 1970, and the average household makes twelve auto trips daily. Habits become ingrained and are hard to break. They are reinforced by the present urban infrastructure designed to exploit the full possibilities of private car mobility.

The underpricing of vehicle travel gives rise to a fifth problem. As we spread out in the region and travel ever greater distances, we must build and maintain ever more roads and bridges. The costs of doing so are further exacerbated by the increasing level of large-truck traffic, which accounts for a disproportionate share of the wear and tear on the infrastructure.

Maintenance costs for the region's road system for the period 1996 to 2020 are expected to total $17.7 billion (in 1995 dollars), funded primarily by the Motor Fuels Tax. The revenue stream from this source has not risen at a rate commensurate with the increased maintenance requirements of the system. As maintenance costs continue to absorb a higher percentage of the budget, the state has fewer funds to devote to capital expansion. Thus, if new revenue sources are not identified, the state is likely to face continued and increasing capital budget shortfalls for the foreseeable future.

> *"No issue is more important in my community than the ability to have a decent job that does not require spending three hours a day in an automobile. . . . It is extremely important to achieve a balance between jobs and housing in any community. Too many jobs result in sterile office parks that are abandoned at nightfall. Too many houses can result in bedroom communities without a central focus."*
>
> ◆
>
> KATHLEEN SEEFELDT, FORMER CHAIRMAN, BOARD OF SUPERVISORS, PRINCE WILLIAM COUNTY, VIRGINIA

THE TRANSIT SYSTEM

The Chicago region is one of a very few in the country that continue to have an elaborate mass-transit system, but unfortunately the region has not come close to tapping the full possibilities of building on this framework and creating a world-class intermodal network for personal mobility.

Public transportation in the six Illinois counties of the region is the operating responsibility of three divisions of the Regional Transportation Authority (RTA) of northeastern Illinois:

▶ The Chicago Transit Authority (CTA) provides bus and rapid-transit service generally within the City of Chicago and to 38 suburban municipalities.

▶ The Commuter Rail Division (Metra) provides commuter rail service connecting downtown Chicago with 68 other Chicago locations and 100 suburban communities.

▶ The Suburban Bus Division (PACE) provides fixed-route bus, paratransit, and vanpool services to 235 communities throughout the suburbs and from suburban locations to the City of Chicago.

The public-transit system's capital assets have a current replacement value of approximately $19.2 billion, but most of its track, bridges, and other structures are at least fifty years old. While the typical equipment life span of these assets is thirty to thirty-five years, the funding reinvestment cycle is currently running at about eighty-five years. The capital needs of the system for the years 1996 through 2020 are projected at $15 billion, to bring the system to a state of good repair, and to maintain it in that state, once achieved. Only $10 billion of this amount is funded in the Regional Transportation Plan (RTP), described in the next section. With a $5 billion shortfall, the transit system can be kept in a safe and usable condition but it cannot be upgraded to enhance its appeal.

The system was originally designed as a hub-and-spoke network to transport workers to the central area of the city. As the city developed outward, the transit system (primarily the CTA) became more limited. As suburban areas grew in population, Metra and PACE experienced small increases in ridership. However, these increases were not nearly enough to offset the huge declines in CTA bus ridership. Due mainly to the tremendous dispersion of jobs and population from sites served by the existing infrastructure, the system's total ridership today is only two-thirds as large as it was in 1970.

During the 1980s, population and employment in the City of Chicago fell by 220,000 and 90,000, respectively. Employment in the city remained level between 1990 through 1995. During this same period, CTA bus ridership continued to decline while ridership on CTA rapid-transit, METRA, and PACE each increased slightly. If the city expects to fulfill the possibly optimistic projection made by NIPC of an 18 percent increase in jobs by 2020, massive investments will be needed in the system to make it the choice of more commuters and leisure-time travelers.

Suburb-to-suburb and city-to-suburb transit needs, which continue to increase, are extraordinarily difficult for the system to meet, owing to low-density land-use patterns and irregular travel times. While vanpool programs grew by 25 percent in 1996, the total number is not significant. A major penetration of the market for these programs will require unprecedented marketing initiatives.

> *"With our congested highways and steadily decreasing mobility, vehicles that are progressively destroying the environment, mass transportation goals that are shortsighted and uncoordinated, and outmoded rail systems that barely make ends meet, it is time we completely rethink each component of our urban transportation network, the relationships and interfaces between them and the inextricable link to the quality of the urban environment we inhabit."*
>
> MOSHE SAFDIE, ARCHITECT

THE 2020 REGIONAL TRANSPORTATION PLAN

In August 1997, the Chicago Area Transportation Study (CATS) issued a comprehensive long-term regional transportation plan entitled Destination 2020 (2020 RTP). CATS is the organization recognized by the United States Department of Transportation as the "metropolitan planning organization" whose plans are prerequisite to the qualification for federal funding of surface-transportation projects in this region.

The 2020 RTP, developed over a three-year period, proposes a coordinated multi-modal ground-transportation system to maintain the region's existing transportation investments and serve its future travel needs through 2020. It is a fiscally constrained plan. The RTA has stated that in addition to the $10 billion (between 1996 and 2020) earmarked by CATS for transit capital maintenance, another $5 billion will be needed to bring the entire transit system to a state of good repair, and the Illinois Department of Transportation (IDOT) has observed that the amounts earmarked for highway capital maintenance ($17.7 billion) will keep the system at the current level of repair but not improve it.

The proposed highway projects would expand the existing expressway-system lane miles by 16 percent (to accommodate the continued outward expansion of the region's growing population) and would expand the rail-transit-system track miles by 14 percent.

The 2020 RTP was a good statement of needed transportation improvements, but it does not constitute a strategic assessment of regional needs. Instead, it consists of a collection of projects that underwent a process of public and technical scrutiny that established some degree of merit but nevertheless reflected the results of a political bargaining process among project sponsors within the CATS forum. Even if all elements of the 2020 RTP are implemented, congestion (by any reasonable measure) will increase markedly.

A greater priority should be given to public transit. The revenues available for funding capital maintenance and new projects for roads and transit in the 2020 RTP (averaging about $1.4 billion per year in 1995 dollars) are inadequate to sustain and improve the regional transportation system. An additional $500 million per year, earmarked primarily for transit projects, must be raised from a combination of taxes and fees directed at the private motor vehicle.

That $500 million per year, together with the bonding authority of the several appropriate governmental units to facilitate front-loading, would bring transit to a state of good repair. Road maintenance could be accelerated, and the unfunded capital projects proposed for further study in the 2020 RTP, many of which are vital to the region, could be built.

Recent suggestions of converting the tollway system to freeways would greatly exacerbate the funding shortfall and should be rejected. To the contrary, future tollway bond indentures should be written to permit tollway revenues, in excess of funding needs, to be used to subsidize mass transit.

Freight Transportation and the Challenge of Intermodalism

While it will take decades to bring about a good intermodal personal mobility system for the region, freight intermodalism on an international scale is already well under way. One of the challenges for metropolitan Chicago is to figure out how it can most profitably exploit its historic position as railway hub of the nation and reposition itself as one of the world's major intermodal centers for the transfer of goods between different rail carriers, between

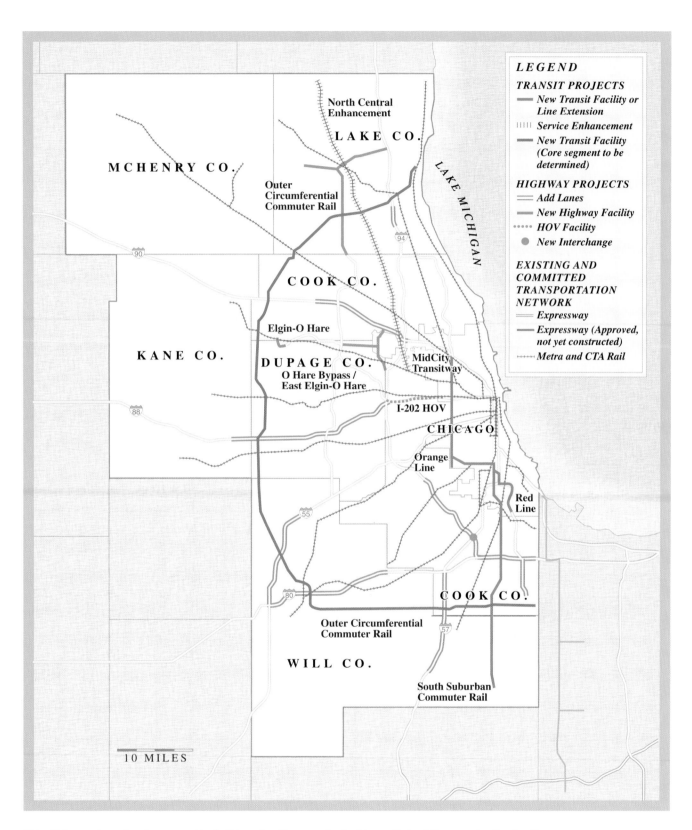

LEGEND

TRANSIT PROJECTS
New Transit Facility or Line Extension
Service Enhancement
New Transit Facility (Core segment to be determined)

HIGHWAY PROJECTS
Add Lanes
New Highway Facility
HOV Facility
New Interchange

EXISTING AND COMMITTED TRANSPORTATION NETWORK
Expressway
Expressway (Approved, not yet constructed)
Metra and CTA Rail

North Central Enhancement

L A K E   C O.

M C H E N R Y   C O.

Outer Circumferential Commuter Rail

LAKE MICHIGAN

C O O K   C O.

Elgin-O Hare

K A N E   C O.

D U P A G E   C O.
O Hare Bypass / East Elgin-O Hare

MidCity Transitway

I-202 HOV

C H I C A G O

Orange Line

Red Line

Outer Circumferential Commuter Rail

C O O K   C O.

W I L L   C O.

South Suburban Commuter Rail

10 MILES

Major highway and transit projects proposed by the Chicago Area Transportation Study's 2020 Regional Transportation Plan (1998).

What life have you if you have not life together?

There is no life that is not in community,

And no community not lived in praise of GOD.

. . . .

And now you live dispersed on ribbon roads,

And no man knows or cares who is his neighbour

Unless his neighbour makes too much disturbance,

But all dash to and fro in motor cars,

Familiar with the roads and settled nowhere.

Nor does the family even move about together,

But every son would have his motor cycle,

And daughters ride away on casual pillions.

. . . .

And the wind shall say: "Here were decent godless people:

Their only monument the asphalt road

And a thousand lost golf balls."

. . . .

Can you keep the City that the LORD *keeps not with you?*

A thousand policemen directing the traffic

Cannot tell you why you come or where you go.

. . . .

When the Stranger says: "What is the meaning of this city?

Do you huddle close together because you love each other?"

What will you answer? "We all dwell together

To make money from each other?" or "This is a community?"

And the Stranger will depart and return to the desert.

O my soul, be prepared for the coming of the Stranger,

Be prepared for him who knows how to ask questions.

T. S. ELIOT, FROM "THE ROCK," 1934

rail and truck, between air transport and both truck and rail, and between water transport and both rail and truck. Chicago, as an intermodal center, is currently defined mostly in terms of its importance as the nation's hub for the transfer of rail cars between railroads and as hub for the transfer of trailers and containers between truck and rail. The intermodal exchange of goods at the region's air terminals and Lake Michigan ports pales by comparison.

The other great challenge in this area is to design a road system that will better satisfy the competing demands of trucks, cars, and buses.

The trucking industry accounts for more than 70 percent of total freight transportation revenues in this country. It has no competitors in the short-haul business, and in intercity movements it accounts for about 55 percent of revenues. Despite the dominance of the trucking industry in recent decades, it would be a mistake to overlook the growing importance of Chicago's legacy as railway hub of the nation and the possibilities for building on this legacy for the future. Now is a good time to look at these possibilities, given the fact that the railroad industry has been enjoying something of a renaissance over the past ten years or so. Its prospects have not been so bright for decades.

CATS, in a July 1997 working paper, estimated the direct and indirect value of the railroad industry to the region's economy (i.e., additions to gross regional product) to be close to $9 billion and growing. These intermodal centers provide jobs, require supplier goods and services, and

Aerial view of the intermodal freight facility at Willow Springs.

offer regional shippers a significant logistics advantage over their competitors from outside the region.

It is in long-haul, intercity freight movement that rail and truck compete, and increasingly they also cooperate. Today, the railroad industry accounts for about 40 percent of this business, up from 35 percent ten years ago. In light of the rebirth of the railroad industry by reason of the growing efficiencies borne of deregulation, consolidations, and new technologies, its share of intercity freight movement should continue to grow over the next ten or twenty years, especially if public-policy changes provide a more level playing field between these two modes of freight transport. Without question, railroads today are the low-cost, long-haul transporters of bulk goods. This is the case even though railroads must own and maintain their own roadbeds while truckers, together with other vehicle users, rely on a road system that is only partially funded by user fees.

The deregulation of the rail industry has made it much more competitive over the last ten years, and the greatest single source of its revenue growth is based on the rail/truck connection. Rail/truck intermodalism has skyrocketed over the last decade. Today, Chicago is not only the nation's most important hub for rail-to-rail transfers; it is also the nation's most important rail/truck intermodal center, accounting for about 5 million lifts (intermodal exchanges of containers and trailers) between rail and truck. This number is expected to grow to 12 million by the year 2020. To put these numbers in perspective, the next most important rail/truck hub in the country is the Los Angeles–Long Beach region with about 3 million such lifts per year.

The most serious remaining obstacle in this region to the efficient movement of goods involving rail-to-rail and rail/truck transfers lies in the time-consuming and costly transfers of rail cars, trailers, and containers from one switching yard to another and between shippers, consignees, and freight hubs. Even though only ten rail carriers (excluding the three carriers that carry out switching and transfer operations in Chicago) move freight to, from, and through Chicago today, they still own and operate more than 100 switching yards, whose consolidation and rationalization would make freight flows more efficient and could increase the amount of land available for other uses.

Rail cars arriving in Chicago for movement to another part of the country must be transferred to another rail carrier. This transfer is usually carried out by delivering the cars to a switching carrier, such as Belt Railway Company of Chicago (BRC) or the Indiana Harbor Belt Railway (IHB), which sorts, assembles, and delivers them to the appropriate connecting carrier at a another railway yard, perhaps a few miles away. The connecting carrier then makes up its train for departure. At best, a rail car arriving the morning of one day is on a train that departs on the evening of the next day. It is not unusual for a rail shipment to be rushed 2,500 miles from California to Chicago in forty-eight hours, only to sit the next forty-eight or more hours tied up in a cross-town transfer.

Where time is of the essence, an incoming carrier needing to switch piggyback trailers or containers may avoid BRC and IHB by delivering them to trucks for transfer by highway to the connecting rail carrier at the other yard. It is estimated that as many as one out of every five trailers and containers passing by rail through Chicago for transfer from one carrier to another is transferred by truck, increasing traffic and the wear and tear on the region's roads.

There are other problems with the switching process. When a train enters the track of another railroad, whether for interchange, tracking rights, or merely crossing, the operator must conform to the yard rules of the host railroad. Unlike air travel, there are no common terminals operated by a dispassionate authority using uniform protocols and imposing rational priorities.

Transportation to and from the Region

AIR TRANSPORTATION

According to the Federal Aviation Administration (FAA), over the next twenty years, Americans will nearly double the number of trips they take per year, thanks to widening job markets, the growing importance of international travel in the age of global markets, far-flung families and attachments, growing discretionary incomes for leisure travel, and a continued shift from cars to planes for long-distance travel.

It would be difficult to exaggerate the economic impact of O'Hare Airport on its surrounding area over the past three decades. In 1989, the O'Hare area (the area within a four-mile radius of the airport, or about 50 square miles) had close to 650,000 jobs, compared with 550,000 in downtown Chicago (3.75 square miles) and 875,000 within three miles of the Loop. O'Hare has in fact changed the regional growth patterns by adding to the employment area that is concentric around the Loop a second one that is concentric around the airport.

The present inability of O'Hare to accommodate the ever-growing demand on its facilities means that we are now losing between three and five fly-overs per day. This loss of operations (take-offs and landings), which is destined to worsen with each passing year, will have significant adverse economic repercussions for the entire region. In addition, capacity at Chicago's point-to-point Midway Airport, one of the largest employers and economic forces on Chicago's south and southwest sides, will reach capacity by 2012. The fact that limits on existing airport capacity in the Chicago region will be reached within the next two decades was recently reconfirmed by an exhaustive study carried out by Booz Allen & Hamilton, as commissioned by the City of Chicago and the Chicagoland Chamber of Commerce.

In the long term, new point-to-point service will be needed beyond what is currently available at Midway. Planning for a third airport began seriously in 1984 when the FAA, in approving the O'Hare expansion plan, required a study to address future demand for the region. In 1986, the IDOT engaged Klynveld Peat Marwick Goerdeler (KPMG) to make an assessment of future needs. KPMG concluded that the region needed a third airport by 2000 and named four sites for further study: Bi-State, Gary, Kankakee, and Peotone.

In 1989, a second study was undertaken by another consulting firm to evaluate the four recommended alternative sites plus Lake Calumet, added at the request of the FAA. Site selection would be made, based on the study, by a policy committee consisting of four Illinois, four Indiana, and three Chicago representatives. In February 1992, this policy committee selected the Lake Calumet site, but the Illinois Senate would not approve legislation enabling Chicago to proceed with development. Later in 1992, the Governor decided to continue with phase two of the study—preparing a master plan and an environmental assessment—focusing on Peotone as the preferred site.

There may be no more dramatic instance of the clash between the general interests of an entire metropolitan region and the special interests of particular segments of the region (here defined to include part of Indiana) than the one posed by the issues of whether and how to expand existing airport capacity and whether and where to build a new airport. Besides the political tensions and stalemates, there are other serious obstacles: a long period of time (eight to fifteen years) is required to plan and develop a new airport; the airlines are generally quite resistant to the addition of a new airport, largely because of high initial costs and scheduling complexities, and also because it eases the entry of new competitors; community concerns over noise generally call for extensive land takings and controls, and these land takings often involve coordination among a number of political jurisdictions, and the opportunities for litigation are rife. Thus, it comes as no surprise that the new Denver Airport is the first major airport to have been built in the United States since the 1974 opening of the Dallas/Fort Worth Airport. In fact, there is not even one new airport proposal that has reached the stage of a firm commitment.

Despite these formidable obstacles, the economic interests of major metropolitan regions are more than ever dependent on capacious airport infrastructures that serve those regions in a balanced manner. Other areas, recognizing both the opportunities and the obstacles, are moving ahead. The Minnesota legislature recently authorized the construction of a new runway and other improvements at the Minneapolis/St. Paul Airport after seven years of study. Dallas and Fort Worth are completing a nine-year project to expand the capacity of their joint airport so as to increase capacity by 75 percent.

HIGH-SPEED RAIL

The high-speed train has a clear competitive advantage over air for shorter trips, says Sir Peter Hall, a professor of urban and regional planning.[2] It has seized "from airlines the great majority of all trips—between 80 and 90 percent—in the distance range between approximately 100 and 300 miles in densely urbanized regions; it functions most efficiently in linear corridors of development such as the Tokaido Corridor of Japan . . . and the eastern seaboard of the United States . . . [it is] likely to play a significant role in maintaining the roles of the traditional urban cores, above all in the major nodal centres."

A number of studies have looked at the feasibility of creating a high-speed, Chicago-hubbed rail network. Such a network would connect Chicago's downtown with those of other major Midwestern cities and link the midsized cities in between. The United States Department of Transportation's Federal Railroad Administration concluded in a 1996 study that Midwest regional high-speed rail development has a higher benefit-cost ratio than any of the other proposed regional rail corridors in the nation.

Because Chicago would be the natural hub of the Midwest network, our area could expect to reap major economic benefits. Also, the network could have a significant effect in reducing traffic congestion and relieving some of the pressure to increase airport capacity. Just as with highways, airports, and waterways, federal funding would be utilized to develop the infrastructure.

LAND USE AND HOUSING

A powerful complex of forces has transformed the metropolitan landscape over the last few decades, and these forces show no signs of abating. One aspect of the transformation is the territorial expansion of the region at a rate far in excess of the rate of population growth and in a manner commonly called "low-density sprawl." The other, sometimes called "social segregation," is the growing division of residents into distinct geographic areas and political units within the region based on their socioeconomic and ethnic or racial characteristics. See appendix B for a brief description of the causes of these two phenomena.

Many would cite the benefits that have been conferred on the majority of households and businesses as a result of the spatial transformation. Households and businesses in the better-off suburbs perceive that they are getting safer and more manageable communities, responsive government, good schools, proximity to nature, clean air, less noise, more housing and land for the money, car access to retail outlets where bulky parcels can be conveniently loaded and taken home to attached garages, better access to skilled labor, lower local taxes, lower land and building costs, plentiful parking, and easy access to airport and truck routes. Many households and businesses in Chicago notice less congestion, more efficient government as the city has engaged in healthy competition with suburbs, lower land costs and increased opportunities for city renewal, and a sharper focus on the postindustrial purposes of cities.

But these benefits have been accompanied by some very serious costs, borne mostly by those living in distressed areas of Chicago and in the worse-off suburbs. Yet, increasingly, many of the costs are being felt by the entire metropolitan region—for example, reduced utility and economic viability of public transportation, increased auto traffic, and reduced air quality; added costs of crime prevention, drug-abuse centers, judicial administration, and prison systems; added infrastructure costs for new roads, sewers, and schools, despite the excess capacity of such infrastructures in older parts of the metropolis, now allowed to deteriorate; loss of a sense of community as people travel great distances to lead their compartmentalized lives at work, home, and play; and loss of valuable agricultural lands and environmentally important open spaces. Worst of all, the spatial transformation has made poverty concentration and social segregation possible on a scale and to a degree unprecedented in the nation's history.

The tragedy is that these costs, for the most part, are not inherent in the dispersal process itself but are rather the consequence of a policy framework that was never designed to accommodate the spatial transformation outlined above. The present mix of governance, tax, and other public policies, and the attitudes of people favoring discriminatory land-use and housing policies, have played a pernicious role in determining the particular lines of dispersal that we have pursued. Changing those policies and attitudes will lead to a more sustainable, efficient, and equitable use of land and the existing infrastructure:

➤ The region will become known not only for downtown Chicago, but also for its several transit-oriented, regional centers outside Chicago—centers with pedestrian-friendly cores and a rich mixture of diverse uses.

➤ The private sector will be encouraged to renew the existing infrastructure of older communities, and it will be discouraged from building new developments that require high-cost, inefficient extensions of the public infrastructure.

➤ The region will be laced with greenways and preserves containing savannas, prairies, forests, floodplains, and wetlands, and the region's rivers and streams will provide many public recreational benefits.

➤ A much wider array of housing opportunities throughout the region will enable people to live in proximity to their work if they so choose, thereby reducing congestion and environmental harm and enhancing productivity.

➤ Government-assisted family housing will provide training and counseling services that enable families to move up and out so that such housing is transitional.

➤ People with disabilities will live in homes that are accessible and affordable, in all parts of the region.

➤ Residents may choose to stay in their home community through each of their various life stages, thanks to a wider choice of available housing options, and no citizen will be denied housing opportunities due to ethnicity or race.

➤ Central city and suburbs will compete, not for tax dollars, but for recognition for excellence in community design and livability.

Sprawl and Its Consequences

Anthony Downs argues that unlimited low-density development has dominated nearly all American policies affecting metropolitan area growth for more than four decades.[1] The chief elements of this dominant vision (tantamount to the American dream), says Downs, are as follows: ownership of detached single-family homes on spacious lots; ownership and unlimited use of automotive vehicles on uncongested roads; employment in low-rise workplaces in attractively landscaped park-like settings, accompanied by spacious, free parking lots; residence in small communities with responsive local governments; and an environment free from poverty.

This vision has been pursued with particular force in northeastern Illinois, where there are no natural physical barriers, other than Lake Michigan, to endless outward expansion. As a result, suburban northeastern Illinois is less densely developed than even Los Angeles.

This dominant vision, Downs says, is badly flawed; *excessive* travel results in congestion, environmental harm, diminished productivity, and reduced time with family, as summarized in chapter 2. Further implications are as follows:

High infrastructure costs. Unlimited low-density development entails infrastructure costs that are far higher per capita than for more compact developments. One study concluded that the street, utility, and school capital costs of noncontiguous, low-density (fewer than three dwelling units per acre), single-family development are more than 50 percent higher per capita than for contiguous development given equal proportions of conventional single-family housing, single-family cluster units, townhouses, garden apartments, and high-rise apartments.[2] Moreover, the excessive building of new fringe-area communities can ultimately lead to the deterioration or even abandonment of much of the existing infrastructure in older communities whose populations are declining. Chicago and inner-ring suburbs have become burdened with abandoned, underutilized, and contaminated commercial and industrial properties known as brownfields. There are approximately 2,000 of these in the city alone.

Loss of open space. Unlimited low-density development entails the excessive loss of farmland and important natural open space. Between the years 1970 and 1990, northeastern Illinois lost 440 square miles of farmland, an amount equal to twice the land area occupied by the City of Chicago. Moreover, new suburban development often encroaches on floodplains.

Construction of the new Sears, Roebuck and Co. headquarters in Hoffman Estates, completed in 1992.

One difficulty facing the biosphere of this metropolitan region is that political boundaries have nothing to do with the location of important features of terrain or resources which need to be shared and safeguarded. The environmental integrity of our region cannot be guaranteed by each of our 270 municipalities acting alone. It is an issue of regional interdependence.

Geographic mismatch between housing and jobs. Middle-income households (those that earn between $30,000 and $50,000 per year) have great difficulty finding housing they can afford, especially if they wish to live in proximity to job growth areas. Between 1980 and 1990, 56 percent of the region's new jobs were located in only 10 percent of the townships. The median home price in these townships was 40 percent higher than the region's median home price. In other words, areas of highest employment growth are also less affordable.

In Lake County, for example, there is a serious shortage of housing for families with incomes up to $50,000. In DuPage County, only half of the demand for housing priced between $80,000 and $125,000 is met. These are homes affordable by households with annual incomes between $30,000 and $50,000, representing more than 27 percent of DuPage's population.

Some would add, as an additional consequence of unlimited low-density development, the loss of community distinctiveness.

Residential Segregation by Race and Income

"The monstrous expansion of cities and urban regions that has been one of the great social features of this century is simply a horror. The phenomenon is worldwide, but there is little uniformity in the forms it takes. . . . In the advanced countries the tendency takes [these] forms: notably, the development of great regions of exurbia and suburbia surrounding the city centers, regions having the drawbacks of both city and country and the virtues of neither. . . . Meanwhile, particularly in our own country, we stand by to witness . . . the reckless raiding and ruining of some of the finest agricultural soil on the world's surface, . . . with the result that we export to other parts of the world great quantities of what, in essence, is our topsoil."

GEORGE F. KENNAN,
FORMER U.S. AMBASSADOR TO
THE SOVIET UNION

The Chicago region has a rich legacy of ethnic neighborhoods dating back to the nineteenth century. These settlements were largely created through a process of self-selection, and they became important mechanisms for mutual support, job networking, and social connectedness for newly arriving immigrants from all over the world. This section is concerned with that other form of segregation that is imposed or induced from outside the segregated community, by legal and/or nonlegal means. By far the most extreme example is the geographic separation of African American peoples from all other ethnic or racial groups.

Three-fourths of the region's African Americans live in Chicago, which accounts for 6 percent of the region's land area and 38 percent of its total population. Blacks constitute nearly 40 percent of the population of the city, and 80 percent of all Chicago's blacks live in only 20 of its 77 community areas. The average degree of black concentration in these 20 communities is over 95 percent. Two-thirds of all suburban blacks live in just 18 of Chicago's 269 suburban municipalities, and 13 of those 18 cities and villages are over 50 percent black.

Residential segregation by income is on the increase. In 1989, the average per capita income of residents in the three richest neighborhoods of Chicago (Lincoln Park, the Loop, and the Near North) was about ten times that of the residents in the three poorest neighborhoods (Grand Boulevard, Riverdale, and Oakland), almost double the multiple for 1979. Likewise, in 1989, the average per capita income of the three richest suburbs (Glencoe, Kenilworth, and Winnetka) was about ten times that of the residents of the three poorest suburbs (Ford Heights, Harvey, and Robbins), up from a multiple of five for 1979. Finally, between 1979 and 1989, the average per capita income of the three richest suburbs, as a multiple of that of the three poorest neighborhoods in Chicago, increased from eight to fifteen.

The Special Housing Needs of People with Disabilities

People with disabilities throughout the metropolis are experiencing a critical housing shortage. This situation is caused by three factors: (1) inadequate accessibility, (2) a lack of affordable options, and (3) discrimination.

The first is the most easily understood—much of Chicago's housing is old and/or inaccessible. Less than 35 percent of all accessible units are occupied by individuals in need of accessible housing, while thousands of disabled people remain on waiting lists for these buildings. Frequently these waiting lists do not take accessibility needs into account.

Inaccessible design is often the result of ignorance of federal statutes and noncompliance with the Fair Housing Amendments Act's accessibility guidelines.

Lack of housing adjacent to potential jobs is a severe problem, and frequently the accessible units are in the more expensive areas not affordable to the majority of people with disabilities. Employment statistics indicate that, compared to nondisabled people, a much higher proportion of disabled individuals earn incomes at or below the poverty level.

There is a history of discrimination, segregation, and extreme isolation for people with disabilities. Some worry that people with disabilities will make other tenants uncomfortable, damage walls and furniture if they use wheelchairs or other medical or mobility devices, require an unusual amount of attention, demand accommodations, and not be able to pay their mortgages or rent. Discriminatory rental and mortgage practices are not uncommon.

Hyperconcentrated Poor Minorities

The great social challenge to our region is posed by the high levels of concentrated poverty and racial and social segregation. True, as African Americans struggled to achieve greater opportunity to improve their job skills and enter the mainstream, they made stunning progress in the workplace.

Yet, over the last two or three decades, the plight of poor minorities in the city and certain inner-ring suburbs has worsened significantly, as noted in the introduction.[3] The new jobs in the outer suburbs often are inaccessible except by private motor vehicle and require skills that the poor do not have. Further, many municipalities use their zoning ordinances and building codes to block the construction of affordable housing in proximity to the new entry-level jobs.

Finally, there are the disastrous consequences of the Public Housing Act of 1949, which instituted and funded the massive public housing projects of the 1950s and 1960s in the United States' largest cities. Little did the policymakers dream that these projects would become permanent warehouses for the minority poor.

Surely, this program represents one of the greatest failures in domestic public policy of the last fifty years. Nowhere has the extent of that failure been more evident than in Chicago. As of late 1998, the Chicago Housing Authority (CHA) owned about 40,000 public housing units, of which 26,000 were occupied and 6,000 were available for occupancy. Most of the 26,000 occupied units, 90 percent of whose occupants are black, are contained in a handful of grim, mostly high-rise buildings clustered on the near south, near north, and near west sides of the city. In addition, the CHA administers over 23,000 other apartment units under the Section 8 certificate and voucher programs.

In the region as a whole, there are roughly 150,000 subsidized units, of which about 100,000 are in Chicago. Thus the CHA manages less than half of the total subsidized units

> *"There are two primary alternatives to sprawl as we know it: better planning of how we use our land; and using—or reusing— the capacity of older neighborhoods, towns and downtowns to a greater extent than they are used now. Both alternatives are essential if we are to successfully manage growth . . . and thus contain sprawl before it bankrupts us socially as well as financially."*
>
> RICHARD MOE AND CARTER WILKIE, *CHANGING PLACES*

TABLE 3   Number of Local Governments by Type in Northeastern Illinois, 1957–1997

	1957	1977	1997
Municipalities	200	261	267
Townships	114	113	113
Special Districts	365	519	587
School Districts	299	315	303
Counties	6	6	6
Total Governments	984	1,214	1,276

Source: U.S. Census Bureau, Census of Governments

in the region. The rest are managed by the housing authorities of the six counties and by a host of nonprofit and for-profit owners. As large as is the total of subsidized units, there are about 3.5 families eligible for subsidized housing for every family fortunate enough to be accepted. These other households must find their way in the private rental market, often by doubling up in older, rundown units, the bulk of which are in Chicago.

In 1998 Congress enacted a new law requiring demolition of all CHA units where the cost of fixing and managing them compares unfavorably to the alternative costs of the voucher program. A very substantial portion of the units fail under this test and are scheduled for demolition. The households affected will be given vouchers and told to find housing in the private housing market; or to the extent the CHA receives federal funding, newly constructed units will be offered to these residents.

During the 1980s, rents rose faster than incomes, and the supply of affordable rental housing decreased through abandonment, demolition, condominium conversion, and price increases. In Chicago, low-income renters lost access to 125,000 low-priced units.

As federal policy moves toward increased reliance on vouchers, government faces the overwhelming obstacle of how to increase the supply of housing for the increasing number of voucher holders. The institutional impediments to builders who stand ready to meet the demand for such housing are several: zoning and lot-size requirements; the widely and strongly held belief throughout the region that rental housing brings in an unsavory element; inadequate counseling of voucher holders to prepare them as responsible inhabitants of private-sector housing; and the bias against developments that might have an adverse effect on the locality's tax base.

GOVERNANCE AND TAXATION

*T*he challenges described in the prior chapter have all been rendered much more daunting by virtue of a governance and tax system in which hundreds of autonomous municipalities within the region compete for property tax base. Local officials are powerfully motivated to employ exclusionary building and zoning code restrictions in order to maintain homogeneous communities and to maximize their tax revenues while minimizing the added cost of government services such as providing schools. Zoning restrictions usually include large-lot zoning for single-family units, extensive floor-area requirements, and limited zoning for multifamily units, especially multifamily units with more than two bedrooms. Most of these restrictions work in tandem to increase the cost of residential developments, which in turn dictates the minimum income a household will need to live in that area. In addition, when restrictive regulations exist within several adjacent communities, sizeable portions of entire income groups can be effectively excluded from a whole subregion.

The financial rewards to a municipality that aggressively pursues the annexation of land and has highly selective development policies can be enormous. These rewards derive from minimizing the number of resident households with school-age children, maximizing the number of high-income households and the amount of high-value commercial space, and privatizing large amounts of open space. Communities that happen to be situated near an important expressway interchange or near O'Hare Airport and that are therefore attractive sites for commercial and retail operations will likely enjoy a per capita property and sales tax base many times that of communities without these advantages. Communities that fail in the competition for high-value development must anticipate the prospect of overcrowded schools, underfunded municipal services, and consistently high property tax rates.

Municipal governments vigorously defend their practical monopoly over development decisions. They argue that the rules for land-use regulation have been well established by the legislature and Illinois' courts, and that the significant impacts of most land-use decisions are, indeed, local—for example, the impact on property values or on municipal revenues and costs.

For their part, private developers have appealed to the state for relief when hindered by what they regard as excessive local regulation (i.e., overly restrictive zoning). Developers also tend to oppose coordinated intergovernmental planning. They prefer to negotiate with more than one municipality or county for the most favorable annexation and development terms rather than be faced with prior intergovernmental agreements—on boundaries, uses of land, donations, impact fees, and building standards—that effectively prevent such bargaining.

Little if any pressure has been put on state government to intervene in the locally controlled system of land annexation and development because of the mutuality of interests among expanding municipalities, local landowners, and developers. But that must change, or the continued cumulative effect of many municipalities making the same kinds of decisions over many years will be extremely harmful to the interests of the region as a whole.

For example, if one municipality declares its desire to remain exclusively a place for large-lot single-family residences except for a new industrial park intended to improve its tax base, little harm is done. If many municipalities follow this same course of action, the cumulative effects are to limit the availability of housing for middle- and lower-income households throughout the region, to exacerbate the geographic mismatch between jobs and housing, to reduce the utility and economic viability of public transportation, to increase auto traffic, to reduce air quality, and to accelerate the loss of valuable agricultural lands and environmentally important open spaces. The most socially distressed suburbs are hit with declining tax bases as residents and businesses locate in communities with a more favorable combination of high tax base, low tax rates, and high-

> "I am not one who believes that flying saucers carry creatures from other solar systems who poke curiously into our earthly affairs. But if such beings were to arrive, with their marvelously advanced contrivances, we may be sure we would be agog to learn how their technology worked. The important question, however, would be something quite different: What kinds of governments had they invented which had succeeded in keeping open the opportunities for economic and technological development instead of closing them off? Without helpful advice from outer space, this remains one of the most pressing and least regarded problems."
>
> JANE JACOBS,
> THE ECONOMY OF CITIES

quality services. The frequent result is a vicious downward spiral: the distressed locality is forced to raise its tax rates and/or reduce important services, and this then encourages even more businesses and residents to consider relocating.

Governance

There are nearly 1,300 units of local government in our region, including 6 counties, 113 townships, 267 municipalities, 303 school districts, and 587 special districts (single-purpose governments). This amounts to about one unit of government for each 6,000 people, five times the ratio in the greater Los Angeles region and seven times the ratio in New York City. This is not to suggest that our problems would suddenly be solved if only we reduced the number of local governments. The central problem is not the inefficiencies that arise out of the proliferation of governmental units, though surely there is ample opportunity for efficiency gains, particularly in the case of the 558 special districts. The key problem, rather, is the bias in our governance and tax framework that encourages localities to compete among themselves for high-value land development. This bias is vastly exacerbated by the sheer number of autonomous governmental units in the region and the lack of a coordinating mechanism with significant authority to address regional issues.

GENERAL APPROACH TO GOVERNANCE REFORM

We reject the notion of metropolitan government, both as a matter of principle and also on grounds of practicality. Experts have debated for decades the merits of different forms of metropolitan government,[1] and some have even pointed to the need for a new federal constitutional convention to transform the country's major metropolitan areas into new states. While a few regions in the United States and Canada have developed limited forms of metropolitan government, primacy should be given to local government, and governmental units having regionwide powers should be established only to deal with critical regionwide issues.

The overarching principle in the development of these recommendations is timeless, and it applies to complex organizations and governments of any kind. It is sometimes referred to as the principle of subsidiarity: "the notion that action should be taken at the lowest level of government at which particular objectives can adequately be achieved."[2] More specifically, matters of local responsibility should be borne by local governments that are close to their constituencies. The corollary to that principle is that regional and state authorities should perform truly regional roles in regard to the governance of the region: first, they should have responsibility for those matters that are clearly regional in scale and cannot be effectively addressed by any locality (for example, regional transportation infrastructure systems); second, with respect to those matters that are primarily local but that are likely to have a substantial impact on other parts of the region, there should be a framework that provides strong incentives toward the making of local decisions that will be consonant with the larger good of the region.

The great virtue of the present governance structure is that it enshrines the principle of subsidiarity. Its weakness is that it fails to observe the corollary principle. The system of local government has long been in place in this country. In an earlier time, with widely scattered cities and villages across the country, each locality could govern its affairs with little or no regard for its distant neighbors. But in a region of 7.7 million residents living in 6 counties and 270 municipalities, in a region whose children attend schools in 306 school districts, such a fragmented system, without unifying structures, is inadequate. It does not take account of the interdependencies of the different parts of the metropolitan area and the need for coordination and cooperation in respect to regional issues.

Consider, by contrast, the business corporation that must pursue its profit objectives within the constraints of a policy framework that has evolved over the last hundred years or more. This regulatory framework requires enterprises to take into account an extensive array of social interests on which their operations impinge—for example, product safety, safety in the workplace, rights of employees and retirees, the integrity of the environment, and the interests of stockholders. No one today could well argue that we do not need this regulatory web of social protection. Indeed, it is this framework, despite all its blemishes, that has made capitalism sustainable and viable over the long term.

Unfortunately, we do not have a comparable kind of framework requiring municipal corporations to take account of an analogous array of social interests in the process of levying taxes, attracting new development, and designing and implementing their zoning, building, and housing codes. Each local government is able to act autonomously, without regard to the adverse effects of its decisions on the larger region.

EXISTING MECHANISMS FOR REGIONAL COOPERATION

The Illinois Constitution provides a mechanism for regional cooperation by granting broad authority for local governments to enter into intergovernmental agreements pertaining to any activity for which the participating governments have individual authority. Local governments have entered into hundreds of agreements addressing such disparate topics as water supply, wastewater treatment, solid-waste management, flood control, fire and police protection, joint purchasing, revenue sharing, and future municipal boundaries. In a few cases these agreements have resulted in legislatively based joint-action agencies with the powers to plan, build, and operate their own public facilities.

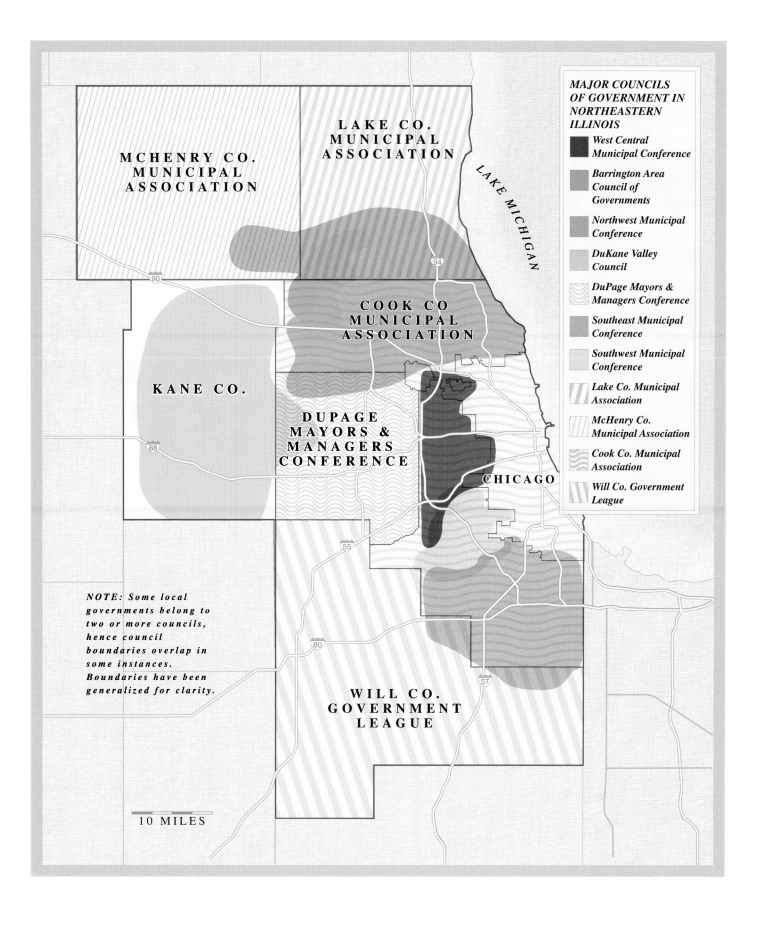

MAJOR COUNCILS
OF GOVERNMENT IN
NORTHEASTERN
ILLINOIS

West Central
Municipal Conference

Barrington Area
Council of
Governments

Northwest Municipal
Conference

DuKane Valley
Council

DuPage Mayors &
Managers Conference

Southeast Municipal
Conference

Southwest Municipal
Conference

Lake Co. Municipal
Association

McHenry Co.
Municipal Association

Cook Co. Municipal
Association

Will Co. Government
League

MCHENRY CO.
MUNICIPAL
ASSOCIATION

LAKE CO.
MUNICIPAL
ASSOCIATION

LAKE MICHIGAN

COOK CO
MUNICIPAL
ASSOCIATION

KANE CO.

DUPAGE
MAYORS &
MANAGERS
CONFERENCE

CHICAGO

NOTE: Some local
governments belong to
two or more councils,
hence council
boundaries overlap in
some instances.
Boundaries have been
generalized for clarity.

WILL CO.
GOVERNMENT
LEAGUE

10 MILES

A number of intergovernmental agreements have been inspired by the region's several municipal associations. Since these associations tend to be organized within county boundaries, many of the resulting agreements are confined to areas within a single county. Thus, they are instances not of regional but of subregional cooperation.

REGIONAL AUTHORITIES OR COUNCILS

The intergovernmental agreement has limited potential as a device for addressing major regional issues. A mechanism with far greater but as yet unrealized potential is the regional council. While many metropolitan areas have established a single, comprehensive intergovernmental organization, this region continues to rely on two specialized agencies with planning responsibility for regional needs. These are the Chicago Area Transportation Study (CATS) and the Northeastern Illinois Planning Commission (NIPC). Their mandates partially overlap.

Since their origins in the 1950s and 1960s, respectively, CATS and NIPC have greatly matured, gaining a more realistic understanding of the region's needs and opportunities as well as of their own institutional capabilities and limitations. Both have greatly improved their analytical skills, whether estimating future motor-vehicle travel or future flood storage capacity requirements. Even so, these agencies will have to overcome serious obstacles before they can achieve the level of effectiveness their missions require.

The original CATS organization covered only the inner third of the region and was limited in scope to planning only for a system of future expressways. CATS prepared its first plan during the late 1950s on the basis of what proved to be greatly overstated regional growth assumptions. The plan could make no reference to a larger policy or comprehensive planning framework because no such framework existed at that time.

CATS' initial plans were never implemented. Its expressway proposals were simply too expensive, both in dollars and in political and social terms. Most of the dollar costs were associated with proposals to build additional major expressways through long-established communities as had been done in the case of the Eisenhower, Kennedy, Stevenson, and Dan Ryan Expressways. When the proposed crosstown expressway failed to be implemented, most other proposals for urban expressway corridors were likewise shelved. Suburbanites also have often blocked new expressways, such as the proposed Fox Valley Expressway. The exception is the North-South Tollway, a suburban expressway that was recommended by CATS and has been partially implemented. Proposed extensions are still under study.

NIPC, too, was extremely limited in its early days, both by the scarcity of funding and by politics, to the point that several years passed before it was able to prepare the comprehensive and functional plans called for in its enabling legislation. NIPC's initial plans promoted compact suburban growth mainly along public-transportation corridors, a design concept strongly endorsed in this report. Since NIPC's plans are only advisory, and it has no executive powers, this initial comprehensive plan could not win the approval of the many municipalities who had their own agendas and had no incentive to consider the region's needs as a whole.

Both agencies have since progressed to the point where their plans and policy recommendations are taken seriously by state agencies and by local units of government. For example, the establishment by the Illinois Department of Transportation (IDOT) of the Strategic Regional Arterial Highway system and IDOT's subsequent roadway improvements were pursuant to the planning efforts of CATS. In the case of NIPC, the most recent example has been the broad acceptance of the Regional Greenways Plan, developed jointly by NIPC and the Open Lands Project.

A third agency, the Regional Transportation Authority (RTA), is not primarily a planning agency, although one of its functions is to coordinate operating and capital expenditures among its three service boards that operate the public transit systems in the region: CTA, Metra, and PACE. The RTA has the unenviable task of maintaining and expanding public transportation services in a region that continues to pursue low-density development, thereby undermining the viability of most forms of public transit. The RTA is empowered to carry out a regional planning and coordination function for public transportation, but it does not pursue this function with vigor. For instance, one of the RTA's widely discussed objectives was to develop a regional fare and transfer policy. This has not yet been accomplished. The RTA does a creditable job of exercising financial oversight over the three operating entities. It also acts as a conduit for the regional sales tax and for state and federal operating and capital subsidies.

The relationships among CATS, NIPC, and the RTA have been outlined in an interagency agreement and by their federal, state, and local funding sources. Consequently, there is little duplication of activities. But the very fact of the fragmentation of planning functions among these agencies has weakened their capacities to address complex issues involving intricate connections between transportation and land-use policy.

The problems with CATS and NIPC also arise out of their resource limitations and their lack of implementation authority. Each of them can engage in facility planning, but neither has the ability to directly implement its own plans or to assure that the results of its efforts will not be undercut by the actions of other governments. For example, the Illinois Toll Highway Authority is not legally required to defer to the plans developed by CATS.

NIPC's level of funding places it on a par with some of the country's smaller metropolitan planning agencies even though its challenges are far more complex. Moreover, NIPC's dependence upon voluntary contributions and consulting contracts often places it in conflict-of-interest positions (for example, when it is asked to review a policy, plan, boundary change, or state or federal grant request submitted by one of its funding sources). Even so, a number of suburban governments have argued that NIPC has interfered with their authority to plan and regulate development as they see fit.

Finally, at both NIPC and CATS, the political bargaining process continues to compete with objective policy analysis for the control of agency decisions. Such competition is to be expected, but political bargaining should be informed by all relevant facts, by the best available analytical tools, and by competent professionals who are insulated from the possibility that the political implications of their advice will determine future agency funding.

WASTEWATER SERVICES

The importance of the region's network of utilities in shaping suburban expansion cannot be overstated. In particular, the provision of sewers and related wastewater treatment services have largely defined when and where suburban expansion has occurred.

In the Chicago area, local sewer systems are generally constructed by land developers and then dedicated to the municipality or county having local land-use jurisdiction. The collection and treatment of wastewater may be provided by a municipality, sanitary district, private utility, or, in the case of Lake County, the county government. If a property lacks access to a wastewater treatment system, whether public or private, the remaining option is to provide on-site disposal, an option often employed in low-density, residential developments in unincorporated areas where each home is provided with its own septic system.

In some parts of the country, a popular strategy for containing suburban sprawl is to create a regional authority to determine the limits of wastewater service areas in keeping with an overall growth strategy. In northeastern Illinois, a process of this type, although limited as to enforceability, was established by the Illinois Environmental Protection Agency (Illinois EPA). As an outgrowth of the federal Clean Water Act, that agency designated facility planning areas (FPAs) within which designated local governments were allowed to provide wastewater collection and treatment services. But the Illinois EPA has recently announced its intention to eliminate the concept of FPAs, which means that there will be no state or regional oversight in northeastern Illinois respecting the expansion of suburban growth through the extension of wastewater services except for the Illinois Commerce Commission's regulation of private utilities. Clearly, a comprehensive state policy is needed with respect to governing the extension of wastewater services and such related matters as storm-water management, water supply, the protection of critical open spaces, the premature development of prime agricultural lands, and the containment of suburban sprawl.

Taxation

The plan focuses primarily on the local property tax and secondarily on the state and local sales tax, the taxes that give rise to most of the fiscal disparities among the different parts

---

TABLE 4   Disparities in Homeowner Property Taxes in Chicago and Suburban Cook County
(1994 property taxes on a hypothetical $100,000 home)

Kenilworth (Cook)

    Tax base, per household . . . . $434,036 . . . . . ('96 EAV* per capita = $55,274)

    Average taxes on home . . . . 2,668 . . . . . ('96 average tax rate = 8.179)

Maywood (Cook)

    Tax base, per household . . . . $48,769 . . . . . ('96 EAV per capita = $5,463)

    Average taxes on home . . . . 4,672 . . . . . ('96 average tax rate = 14.352)

Chicago (Cook)

    Tax base, per household . . . . $83,884 . . . . . ('96 EAV per capita = $11,307)

    Average taxes on home . . . . 2,716 . . . . . ('96 average tax rate = 8.872)

Source: "Mapping the Future," p. 9
*Equalized Assessed Value

of the region and create the most serious hurdles in the way of achieving the plan's economic and social goals.

THE LOCAL PROPERTY TAX SYSTEM

The property tax is by far the most important source of revenue for local governments of every variety, and it is the only significant local funding source for school districts. Because localities are entitled to fund their operations by levying a tax on the assessed value of their respective property tax bases, there are wide disparities in education funding, as noted in chapter 1. Moreover, as discussed earlier, local governments have perverse incentives under the system to compete for high-end residential and commercial developments and shun the development of affordable housing, especially housing for middle- and low-income families with school-age children. The cumulative effects are serious.

Cook County is the only county in the state that uses differing percentages of value in arriving at assessments for various categories of property. In addition, there is a systemic undervaluation of residential property in Cook County. For example, residential property is assessed in Illinois, on average, at 9 percent of market value compared to a statutory 16 percent rate in Cook County. As a result, the state imposes a high equalization factor to all categories of property in Cook. Briefly, this classification system results in overassessments on business properties and underassessments on residential properties. All other counties assess, or at least purport to assess, all properties at a uniform percentage of value. As a result, a business located in Cook may pay property taxes that are three or more times what it would pay if its operations were located in one of the collar counties.

STATE AND LOCAL SALES TAXES

Local governments rely on the property tax and state aid as their primary sources of revenues. But local sales taxes are also important for many cities. The state's general sales and use tax is a tax on the retail sales of various goods, excluding (most notably) food for home consumption and drugs, that disproportionately impacts the poor. It does not cover services of any kind. Yet, services comprise an increasingly important component of personal expenditures in today's economy. They are purchased disproportionately by middle- and upper-income households, but are currently excluded from the tax base. Generally, the current statewide tax rate is 6.25 percent, and the state keeps 5 percent. Of the remaining 1.25 percent, 1 percent is returned to the municipality and .25 percent is returned to the county where the revenue is generated.[3] The state also collects a regional sales tax (levied at various rates in the six-county region, but at an average rate of .25 percent), which it turns over to the RTA. Home-rule governments may impose an additional sales tax in .25 percent increments to purchases within their boundaries. By comparison to other states, Illinois has a relatively narrow sales tax base and a relatively high state-imposed rate. Only four states have a higher rate than Illinois' rate of 6.25 percent.

CRITERIA FOR EVALUATING TAX SYSTEMS

A tax system should be evaluated in reference to the following criteria:[4]

1. *Efficiency.* An efficient tax is one that is designed to minimize distortions of economic decisions by defining broad tax bases and setting low marginal tax rates. An extension of this criterion involves making the payers of the tax and the users of the services financed by that tax the same set of persons, insofar as possible. This may entail taxes on items or activities that result in costs to society at large. Implicitly, the efficiency criterion calls for a tax system that does not put the state or the region at a competitive disadvantage vis-à-vis other states and regions. It also implies accountability, linking the authority to spend to that for raising revenues.
2. *Equity.* An equitable tax imposes equal tax burdens on individuals in the same or similar circumstances (horizontal equity) and imposes differing degrees of tax burdens based on differing abilities to pay (vertical equity).
3. *Simplicity.* A simple tax is one that is easy to administer and one that affords easy understanding and compliance for the taxpayer.

In addition to these primary criteria, a tax system should be stable and responsive. A stable system weathers economic storms well. A responsive system reflects economic growth well. Finally, the tax system should be considered in its entirety in light of these criteria, not on a piecemeal basis.

Aerial view of Woodfield Mall in Schaumburg.

Needless to say, no tax system has yet been devised that meets all of these criteria. In developing any tax-reform proposal, trade-offs must be made. With taxes that fund education, for example, we should be willing to sacrifice on the scores of efficiency and simplicity to achieve the equity that the current system clearly has not achieved: all children should have an equal chance for a better life. But, in general, to the extent the designers of a tax-reform proposal take these criteria seriously, the confidence of taxpayers in the system and the competitiveness of the regional economy are enhanced.

POLICY CONCERNS IN LIGHT OF THE CRITERIA

In 1995, $12.9 billion in property taxes was collected by local governments in Illinois, more than double the amount of revenue from the state sales tax and nearly double the amount from the individual income tax. Property tax revenues in Illinois are about 20 percent higher than the national average on a per capita basis. Excessive reliance on the local property tax, as presently constituted, exacerbates resource inequities among localities and school districts; it generates intergovernmental conflict; it has perverse effects on economic development; and it contributes to flight from the city and to sprawl. However, as has been noted, these consequences have much more to do with the manner by which the tax base is allocated among districts than its actual size.

THE LOCAL PROPERTY TAX AND EDUCATION FUNDING

Historically, the property tax has been one of the most difficult of all taxes to administer, given the multiplicity of assessing and taxing bodies. While the techniques of assessment have improved markedly in recent decades, especially in regard to residential properties, the assessment process will never be an exact science. What is the value of a Sears Tower?

Property value is initially determined in the five collar counties by township assessors and in Cook County by the county assessor. The assessment process is complex, and competition among assessment districts results in pressure on assessors to undervalue property. State boards of equalization have not been successful in stopping politically motivated undervaluation. In addition, the appeal procedure is cumbersome and usually requires an initial appeal within the county. Although ultimately taxpayers have the right to take their case to court, the process is daunting. Before going to court, the taxpayers must pay the tax, and even then, the burden of proof remains on their shoulders.

On the other hand, the tax has some features that make it especially suitable to supporting the large number of overlapping taxing units that exist in the region. Every parcel of real estate is visible, in a fixed location, and even the smallest governmental unit has taxable property within its jurisdiction. Because the tax is levied against the property, not a person, it is unnecessary to know or locate the owner to levy the tax. And collection is relatively easy, because taxes are a lien on property, and good title to property cannot be issued until all outstanding taxes are paid.[5]

One of the chief virtues of the property tax system is its ability to weather economic storms. It provides a comparatively stable stream of revenue in good times and bad. Also, as the economy expands and the need for more services arises, wealth (and therefore the tax base) tends to rise. Thus it rates high on responsiveness.

In some respects the property tax is highly efficient in that it acts much like a benefit tax or user fee for consumers of local services such as police and fire protection. More generally, it has been argued that the property tax in a metropolitan area having many municipalities is a highly efficient tax. The argument is that competition among local governments results in an efficient allocation of public resources; that the threat of out-migration of residents forces local governments to produce government goods and services at minimal cost; that residents are enabled to select the preferred mix of public goods and services among the many being offered; and that residents willingly pay the price of admission (the property tax) because they have chosen the service/tax bundle they most desire.

But the local property tax, particularly as a source of funding education, fails miserably under the equity criterion. As aggregate property wealth has increased and generated large increases in tax revenues for many or most schools in the region, the percentage of total school funding accounted for by state funding sources has diminished. With the state's decreasing role in funding education, 62 percent of local property taxes, totaling over $6 billion, is now devoted to financing the public schools in the six-county region. The extreme disparities in per student spending arise out of this growing reliance on the local property tax and the decentralized, fragmented system of local school districts, with their widely varying levels of per capita property wealth.

Section 1, article 10 of the Illinois Constitution of 1970 provides: "A fundamental goal of the People of the State is the educational development of all persons to the limits of their capacities. The State shall provide for an efficient system of high quality public educational institutions and services."

The legislature and the courts have not come close to taking this constitutional mandate seriously. In a 1996 case the Supreme Court of Illinois noted that during the 1989–90 school year, the average tax base in the wealthiest 10 percent of elementary schools was more than thirteen times the average tax base in the poorest 10 percent. In March 1996, six months before its decision in that case, the Report of the Governor's Commission on Education for the State of Illinois found glaring disparities in school support figures. Property wealth per pupil ranged from $5,000 in poor districts to $1.2 million in wealthy districts.

Despite these egregious facts, the court held that questions relating to the quality of education are solely for the legislative branch to answer because courts are incapable of defining "high quality public educational institutions and services," and that solutions to problems of educational quality should emerge from a spirited dialogue between the people of the state and their elected representatives. In a lone dissenting opinion, Justice Charles Freeman wrote: "Out of fear of entering a 'political thicket' . . . the majority completely abdicates its constitutional duty to interpret the Illinois Constitution."

In 1997, the state legislature amended the education laws to provide a more adequate floor for school funding, as described in chapter 1, but there continue to be large fiscal disparities among school districts.

THE INEQUITY OF THE SALES TAX SYSTEM

How does the present sales tax system measure up against the criteria set forth above? In general, a sales tax system compares favorably with an income tax or property tax in terms of simplicity and ease of administration. Even here, however, the growth of electronic commerce that is free of sales taxes has put local retailers at a disadvantage. And under the remaining criteria, particularly that of equity, it comes out poorly.

The unfairness of this tax in a densely populated region stems from the radical differences among municipalities in terms of their capacity to generate retail sales. This has been the case ever since the advent of the supermall, which draws from an extended portion of the region. These malls are sited in municipalities where there is easy access to expressways. Those relatively few municipalities that are fortunate to be so located are able to generate many times the sales tax per capita that the other municipalities can generate. For example, between September 1996 and August 1997, the following four municipalities generated sales tax revenues per resident as follows: Oakbrook, $1,167; Schaumburg, $341; Chicago, $59; Brookfield, $30.

TABLE 5   Tax Base, Tax Rates, and Total Resources for Selected School Districts in NE Illinois, 1998–99

	EAV* per Pupil (1,000s)	Local Property Tax Rate	Total Resources per Pupil†
River Grove Elementary	$167,739	2.7%	$6,044
West Northfield Elementary	474,900	1.7	8,537
Winfield Elementary	171,487	2.5	5,131
Gower Elementary	410,561	1.6	7,232
Bloom Township HS	227,635	2.3	9,513
New Trier HS	726,685	1.8	13,927
McHenry HS	320,647	1.6	6,109
Fenton HS	668,038	1.6	11,296

Sources: Illinois State Board of Education and Metropolitan Planning Council
*Equalized Assessed Value
†Includes all local, state, and federal revenues

The other significant problem is the responsiveness of the sales tax to economic growth. One of the fastest growing components of the economy is services, which, as noted, is exempted from the tax base.

THE EXCESSIVE USE OF SUBSIDIES FOR COMMERCIAL DEVELOPMENT

Two types of tax policies are used by state and local government to facilitate economic growth. One is selective tax abatement and special subsidies awarded to industries and, more commonly, to individual firms. The other is a general tax structure that encourages and does not unduly inhibit development. Metropolis 2020 favors the second of these two approaches but supports the use of targeted tax approaches, such as tax increment financing (TIF), where they can be justified on the basis of the remediation of blighted areas that would not otherwise be developed. One problem is that TIF and other special subsidies are often used as general spurs to economic development, even on greenfield sites. Another is that they often benefit new businesses at the expense of existing businesses. Such practices then end up compensating for the deficiencies in the general tax structure when a reform of that structure is by far the preferable course of action. They can also have a negative impact on other taxing districts such as schools.

THE EXACERBATING EFFECTS OF THE COOK COUNTY CLASSIFICATION SYSTEM

Cook County, alone among the counties of Illinois, assesses commercial properties at more than double the percentage of value used for residential property. Specifically, in Cook taxes are levied on various percentages of property value ranging from 16 percent on residences to 38 percent on commercial properties.[6] The other 101 counties levy (or purport to levy) taxes on a uniform percentage of value ($33^1/_3$ percent).

State law mandates that an equalization factor be applied to every county in the state so that the state's aggregate real property tax, on an overall basis for all kinds of property, is $33^1/_3$ percent of assessed value. In recent years the equalization factor for Cook has been over two (in part by reason of the underassessment of residential property), with the result that many businesses in the county have seen their equalized assessed valuation doubled to 76 percent of real value and have ended up paying very high property taxes, especially when compared to businesses located in the suburbs outside Cook County, where all property owners are statutorily assessed at $33^1/_3$ percent and where the equalization factor is usually one. The result is the further exacerbation of competition among localities for commercial development and of flight to other counties, as described above.

THE NEED FOR ADMINISTRATIVE REFORM AND PROFESSIONALIZATION

The time is ripe for administrative reform. We now have a greater than ever capacity to appraise property and to evaluate the results of that process, thanks to the emergence of computer-assisted methodologies. Computerization also gives taxpayers much easier access to information. These new methodologies will require assessors to be board-certified appraisers using national standards for assessment. In chapter 9, we recommend that the assessment function be centralized at the county level (as it now is in Cook) and that the office of assessor be an appointive rather than an elective position as is now the case. To the charge that centralization will violate cherished principles of local autonomy, the answer is that centralizing the purely administrative act of assessment of property removes the grounds for one of the frequent criticisms of the property tax: the lack of uniformity in both the assessment and collection process.[7]

ECONOMIC
WELL-BEING

*T*wenty years ago Jane Jacobs wrote *Cities and the Wealth of Nations.* The point of the title was that cities at their best are the great wealth generators of the nations in which they are located, far out of proportion to the populations they contain. She went on to show why some cities are so much more productive than others and why some fall so suddenly from positions of preeminence. If she were writing such a book today, it would be entitled *Metropolitan Regions and the Wealth of the World,* and she would proceed to explain why our region and perhaps another dozen regions in the world are such unique centers of wealth creation. She would stress again how once-great regions can lose their dynamism, and vice versa.

Over the last fifteen years, the number of jobs in the region grew by nearly 30 percent while the population grew by only 6 or 7 percent. At the end of 1998, the unemployment rate for the region was only 4.5 percent, compared to 6.7 percent a decade earlier. We do not know when another major economic downturn might occur, but there is every reason to believe that over the long term we can continue to grow in jobs and productivity and in terms of quality of life, provided we are not lulled into a false sense of security.

One of the great things about the Chicago region has been its periodic bursts of self-renewal, from the aftermath of the Great Fire of 1871 down to the present time. However, when things are going as well for the vast majority of us as they are today, it is hard to perceive that anything could ever go wrong or to see that there are problems that need fixing before they damage our competitive standing or quality of life and become far more difficult and costly to repair.

> *"The business of the future must be controlled by a somewhat different type of men [and women] to that of previous centuries. . . . The motive of success is not enough. It produces a short-sighted world which destroys the sources of its own prosperity. . . . A great society is a society in which its men [and women] of business think greatly of their functions."*
>
> ⬦
>
> ALFRED NORTH WHITEHEAD,
> *ADVENTURE OF IDEAS*, 1933

An analogy from the corporate world well demonstrates the dangers of complacency. In the early 1980s, when General Motors Corporation still had 45 percent of the car market in the United States, no one could have anticipated that GM was about to be dealt one devastating blow after another, first by Japanese automotive companies and later by Ford and Chrysler, whose viability had been threatened by the economic downturn of 1980–82. While they were taking strong measures to avoid disaster and regain their competitive edge, GM had grown comfortable. By the end of that decade, GM's share of the market was down to 32 percent.

This region is facing a similar challenge. Twenty years hence, if we do the right things now, the region will be one of the ten or fifteen great metropolitan centers of the world economic order that is emerging. If we fail, historians could then look back on metropolitan Chicago as the region that once served as the financial, marketing, and insurance center for the powerful agro-industrial complex of the Midwest but that lost its way in the closing years of this past century because its leaders lacked a sense of vision, because they failed to understand the altered structure of the world economy, and because they failed to develop and act on strategies for adapting to the new order.

One of the chief aims of Metropolis 2020 is to ensure that we do not become comfortable in this current era of unparalleled prosperity. The plan focuses chiefly on the physical and institutional infrastructures and policy frameworks pertaining to transportation, land use and housing, education, governance, and taxation. The economic goals of the plan are to alter these background conditions in ways that will enable and encourage the residents of metropolitan Chicago and its employers to meet the challenges of the new world order in which region competes against region and to bring about a high and sustainable level of prosperity.

The first five challenges, already covered in this plan, are as follows: the need for uniform, regionwide excellence in public education and early child care; the need for state-of-the-art surface and air transportation systems; the need for "smart growth" land-use policies and equitable housing policies; the need for fundamental reform of the state and local tax system; and the need for governance reform.

Three additional challenges are identified in this chapter. As in the case of the first five, these challenges arise out of our changed and changing circumstances. The first five challenges entail strategies that call for implementation efforts stretching out over the next decade or more, but the challenges described in this chapter invoke needs that can be met over the next several years:

A New Approach to Workforce Development

Two decades ago, baby boomers and women were entering the market in record numbers, and the region was about to experience a prolonged recession. Job creation became the great need. That era has long since ended, and in today's vibrant economy the challenge is just the opposite—how to sustain a prosperous region over the next two decades when labor at all skill levels will remain in short supply. This situation calls for a two-pronged approach: strategies for tapping the job potential of the unemployed and underemployed segments of the population; and strategies for enabling persons at all skill levels to upgrade their skills and better adapt to an ever-changing economic order.

ADDRESSING THE NEEDS OF UNEMPLOYED AND WELFARE-DEPENDENT PERSONS

Nearly one-fourth of all persons in the region over age twenty-five (about 1.1 million) do not have a high school degree, and 42 percent of these people have less than a ninth-grade education. Many of them have little or no work experience. Close to ten percent of this population, or about 100,000 adults, are on welfare, and almost all of them live in Chicago. The

recent welfare policy changes, including the new five-year limitation, combined with the growing scarcity of labor, add a new urgency to the need for workforce development programs to lift these people out of poverty and turn them into productive members of society.

The first step may be to place unemployed and welfare-dependent citizens in low-skill, low-wage jobs, but the ultimate aim is to move them into jobs that provide sufficient income to sustain their families. We have a long way to go. Current programs are reaching only a small fraction of the poor, including the working poor. And even though some groups are quite effective in their efforts to help welfare recipients and the unemployed obtain jobs, the percentage obtaining living-wage employment is very low.

Rather than isolating the urban poor in special, stand-alone programs, successful efforts in New York, Chicago, and other cities seek to connect this population to mainstream education and training programs, using "bridge" or pre-apprenticeship training where necessary. In addition, effective initiatives involve a network of providers working in partnership to provide the comprehensive range of services needed to help the unemployed and underemployed secure gainful employment. Training is only one of several support services needed; transportation and child care are also vital, as is assistance in identifying job opportunities and follow-up support to foster job retention and help build a stable work history. Indeed, research on successful workforce development strategies suggests that these services, as well as socialization toward employment, are equally important as or even more important than the skill training itself.

ADDRESSING THE NEEDS OF THE AVERAGE WORKER

Workforce development is not just for the unemployed. The region must also develop better programs to enable practically all job holders to upgrade their skills on a continuous basis. By 2006, nearly 40 percent of the highest skill jobs will require post–high school technical training.

Employers, labor leaders, community and social service organizations, and government all have important and distinct roles to perform in this broader responsibility of continuous education and training, to meet the needs of both the unemployed and the employed. Employers can form connections with social organizations to identify job needs, provide on-the-job training, and help familiarize job entrants with the social organization of the workplace. In addition, employers can provide feedback to policymakers and social service providers, and they can participate in school-to-work programs.

Unions of skilled workers can work more closely with public and parochial schools and community colleges to design programs to open up skilled trades to minorities and new immigrants.

Social service organizations can help workforce entrants through evaluation, coaching, behavioral training, and child daycare, and by connecting appropriately prepared individuals to job opportunities and serving as a liaison to employers. Government can best focus on basic education, on the funding of training programs, on transitional financial support, and on providing a well-functioning job-matching facility.

Job training is the primary obligation of employers. For one thing, employers can adapt and improve upon the "German model," whereby businesses help fashion curriculum and fund secondary "school-to-work"-type programs. Second, business has the opportunity in this region to work much more intimately with community colleges so as to ensure that they are teaching the technical skills that are most in demand in the workplace.[1]

THE NEED FOR SYSTEMIC REFORM

Currently, nearly $600 million is spent each year on public-sector job training in the state, with nearly 50 percent of the funds being channeled to the community college system. Additionally, there are 56 different government funding sources for job training in metropolitan Chicago alone. This highly fragmented "system" creates significant duplication, massive inefficiency, and a web of bureaucratic requirements that are burdensome for all involved: job seekers, service providers, and potential employers. The absence of uniform standards or consistent evaluations makes it impossible to compare results among various programs. Moreover, present performance criteria tend to stress short-term job placement and ignore long-term retention or income gains, heightening the probability that participants will obtain low-wage, dead-end jobs.

Thus, the need is for a comprehensive and coordinated workforce development system that will more effectively draw upon the distinctive resources of employers, labor organizations, community-based organizations, the community college system, myriad state agencies (such as the Department of Employment Security, the Department of Commerce and Community Affairs, the Department of Human Services, the State Board of Education), as well as the Mayor's Office for Workforce Development in Chicago, the Chicago Partnership for Economic Development, and various county agencies across the region.

Preparing the Region for Its New Role in the Economic Order

The new economic order is characterized by global markets, advanced information and communications technologies, and a strong service orientation. In this new order, metropolitan Chicago must go beyond its traditional roles in international trade, banking, tourism, and conventions and meet three conditions. First, it must serve as a site for the coordination and control of complex organizations running dispersed networks of factories, offices, and service and distribution outlets. Large and medium-sized corporations, with

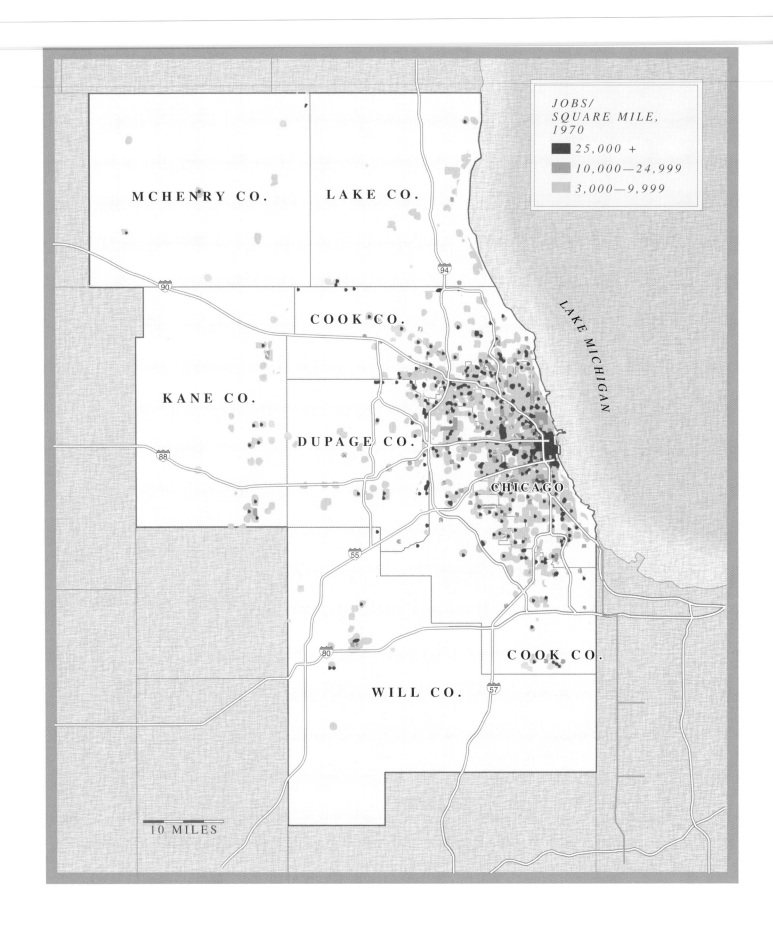

MCHENRY CO.

LAKE CO.

COOK CO.

KANE CO.

DUPAGE CO.

CHICAGO

LAKE MICHIGAN

COOK CO.

WILL CO.

10 MILES

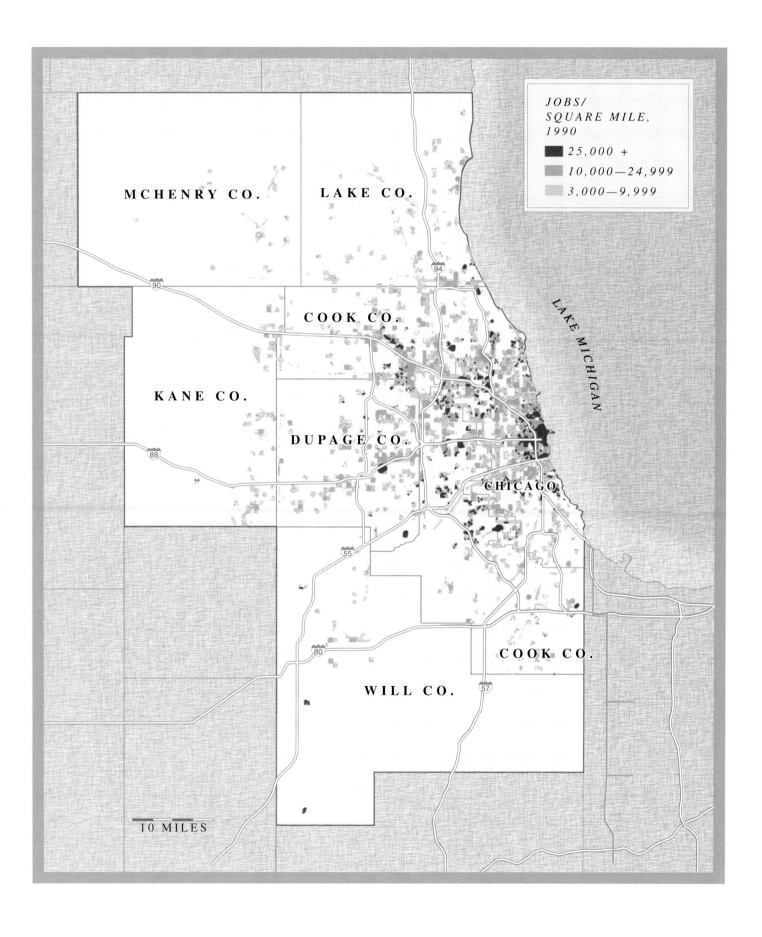

MCHENRY CO.

LAKE CO.

COOK CO.

KANE CO.

DUPAGE CO.

CHICAGO

LAKE MICHIGAN

COOK CO.

WILL CO.

10 MILES

their worldwide span of activities, need to be headquartered in Chicago or in one of the region's other principal centers of business activity with easy access to O'Hare Airport and to a world-class communications infrastructure.[2] These firms rely on a wide variety of specialized service firms that are found mainly in downtown Chicago but also in the other regional centers.

This points to the second condition. Our region must provide the ideal environment in which skilled professionals can provide their crucial inputs into corporate decision-making. Conditions of close proximity facilitate these kinds of creative, subtle interactions among various specialists whose diverse talents must be brought to bear on complex problems. Technology can expand this network but is not likely to replace it.

Third, our region must provide an environment that is hospitable to small and medium-sized corporations and that serves as an incubator of new enterprises. These corporations and startup companies account for all the job growth and most of the innovation in the private sector. Organizational size no longer necessarily confers the competitive advantage that it once did, particularly in the manufacturing sector. In this era of deregulation, smaller, more nimble enterprises whose managers are driven by strong incentives are becoming an ever more important factor.

There are a number of reasons why large enterprises have been restructuring and why there has been a transition from an economy dominated by large, hierarchical, vertically integrated organizations to one that is increasingly characterized by a complex network that connects these restructured corporations and many small and medium-sized firms—a network that best works in a metropolitan area with vital, compact employment centers:

➤ Modern information and communication technologies have enabled the large corporation to radically reduce the numbers of employees required for collecting, storing, retrieving, and transmitting information.

➤ The Internet, wireless communications, and other technologies, combined with organizational innovations, have radically reduced the costs of market transactions between contractors and subcontractors. Consequently, market transactions between a larger number of enterprises account for an increasing share of economic activity, and the share accounted for by hierarchy (i.e., large organizations) is diminishing. For example, over the last ten or fifteen years, the domestic auto industry, under the influence of the Japanese, has been learning how to vertically disintegrate and forge mutually profitable and durable relations with its subcontractors. Other industries have done the same.

➤ As the long-standing advantage of large bureaucracies in minimizing transaction costs has been eroded, their limitations have become more apparent: they tend to stifle innovation and the competitive spirit. The three conditions outlined above will be met only as the cumulative result of pursuing the overall plan embodied in this document.

A Centralized Database and a Marketing Strategy

The development of a regionwide database for analyzing the metropolitan economy and its individual communities is essential for existing and prospective employers seeking hard-to-get information as they decide to locate new or expanded operations in the region. It would also be used to fashion a more detailed, long-term competitive strategy.

And, in order to attract high-level business and professional talent, a far better job of marketing the many advantages of metropolitan Chicago as a place in which to live and work is needed.

Guiding Principles

The plan's approach to economic development is based on certain guiding principles. First, steps toward effective economic development must be led by private-market initiatives, whereas government policies should be designed to maintain a strong general business climate, not to achieve a planned or targeted set of industry-specific goals. Economies are not easily "guided." Indeed, the most zealous of guidance efforts, more often than not, have proved to be counterproductive. In particular, so-called industrial policies, or "picking winners," have failed, and so have efforts in some countries to expand the social safety net too far, thereby distorting individual incentives to save, work, and invest. The increasing importance of the internet and e-commerce only reinforce this lesson.

Second, just as private companies have been forced to become smarter and leaner, regions need to follow suit and develop strategies that better support business and that ensure a high quality of life for their residents. Government must focus more intently on its core functions: education, transportation and communications infrastructures, public safety, and land-use policies. Meanwhile, the business voice in these decisions can help to set the direction of public policies and, especially, to lend continuity across changing government administrations.

A third guiding principle is that strategies for promoting economic development and growth must change to reflect the emerging economic order of the world. To quote Michael Porter,[3] "We must make a transition from thinking of the challenge of cities, and especially of inner cities, as one of reducing poverty. Instead we must redefine the challenge as one of creating income and wealth.... This distinction contains volumes of insight about how one sees the problems and identifies solutions."

This new model focuses on wealth creation through an energized private sector, the integration of the central city with the regional economy, the encouragement of skilled and experienced minorities to build businesses, the enlistment of the private sector to promote

Chicago in the year 2020.
Colored-pencil rendering by
Gilbert Gorski.

economic development, and a government focus on improving the environment for business.

This new model for economic development is not laissez-faire; it recognizes that the private sector must be more engaged with the public sector and also provide direction for the region's development policies. Such leadership is necessary because the private sector best understands the sources of economic growth and the needs and conditions for job creation.

The fourth guiding principle is that continuity and consistency in regionwide public policies are becoming more important across an urban area that is as politically fragmented but as economically integrated as metropolitan Chicago. To be sure, competition among municipalities within a metropolitan region may help to hold down the costs of many public services, and a multitude of community governments allows each of them to choose the mix of public services that best suits their purposes. Similarly, individual communities may do well in fashioning their own unique business structures and climates. However, individual development policies across neighboring jurisdictions can sometimes end up working at cross-purposes. And some of our most important challenges, including educating the region's future workforce and planning a regionwide transportation system and digital communications infrastructure, require a broad geographic perspective on the region's economy. A clear and sustained voice from the business community will assist communities within the region in recognizing their interdependencies and fashioning appropriate policies that benefit both themselves and their neighbors.

PART TWO

RECOMMENDATIONS

The recommendations set forth in part 2 are intended to spark regionwide conversations that will improve upon the plan's ideas and contribute to the development of legislative and private-sector proposals that are likely to win the support of a wide spectrum of civic, political, and business leaders throughout the region.

The recommendations take full account of the strong interconnectedness among transportation, land use, housing, the environment, governance, and taxation. For example:

➤ For decades, thousands of families have departed the city each year and relocated in the suburbs in order to ensure that their children receive a high quality of public education. Most of these families—especially those where one or both parents work in the city—would prefer an environment in which their residential choices were not constrained by educational factors. As the quality of schools in Chicago and the inner-ring suburbs improves and a reverse migration of sorts begins to occur, there will be greater access to public transportation, and the prospects for the long-term viability of the region's public-transit system will be enhanced.

➤ A very substantial portion of all commuters cannot afford to live near their place of work. Land-use reforms to cure this locational mismatch will reduce mobility needs, increase productivity, and enhance the quality of the air.

➤ Tax reforms to price motor-vehicle travel so as to more nearly reflect the true costs of such travel will improve land-use patterns and reduce environmental harm.

➤ Without governance reform, it will be very difficult to address the problems of unlimited low-density development, encourage reinvestment in older blighted areas of the region, and protect open space.

Because this is a strategic, conceptual document, no attempt has been made to quantify either the costs that will be incurred or the savings that will be realized if our recommendations are implemented. Those projections can only be made as definitive proposals are developed in the ensuing years on the basis of the document's strategic guidelines. Nevertheless, it is important to note that this plan, when viewed in its entirety and over the long term, may well not entail a net increase in state and local taxation for the vast majority of households. In the first place, there are offsets to the funding proposals—for example, the recommended increase in vehicle and fuel-related taxes could be more than offset by savings from privatizing transit and other transportation-related services as recommended in chapter 7; and the recommended increase in taxes to provide more equitable access to education and to fund the Regional Coordinating Council proposed in chapter 9 could be substantially offset by the government streamlining initiatives called for in that chapter. In the second place, even though it is unlikely that we will achieve tax neutrality within the first several years of implementation efforts, the residents of the region should expect to enjoy rich dividends from the recommended investments to develop people's skills, to improve the transportation system, to enhance the wise use of natural resources, and to moderate fiscal disparities. These dividends will be realized in terms of increased human productivity, quality of life, and equity of opportunity, and stronger communities.

I N V E S T I N G   I N C H I L D R E N

Public Education

T O W A R D   M O R E   E Q U I T A B L E   T A X   F U N D I N G

Fiscal disparity among school districts is not the only reason for the differing qualities of education in different areas of the state, but it is one of the most important. It would be possible to create a regional authority to moderate fiscal disparities, but education is a state constitutional responsibility, and educational funding reforms should continue to be considered at the state level.

If the goal of greater equity of funding for education were simply substantial equality of funding for all students in the state (a goal that several other states have pursued), and if there were no insuperable political obstacles in the way of achieving that goal, that could be achieved by replacing the local property tax as the principal source of educational funding with a statewide property tax, an increase in the state income tax, a broadened state sales tax on services, a shared sales tax system (as envisioned in chapter 8 as a way of partially funding the Regional Coordinating Council), a share of the tobacco taxes, or some combination of the above. The funds thus raised would be the sole source of school funding, and the funds would be distributed equally among the school districts on a per-student basis, after adjusting for regional cost variations.

This "equality-of-funding" approach was rejected on two grounds. First, many participants in the development of Metropolis 2020 believe that the best approach is not sub-

the lines of the enabling statutes that emulate those governing higher education or, for that matter, the business corporation.

We recommend that the Illinois State Board of Education (ISBE) be restricted, or that it restrict itself, to performing the following functions: (1) establishing rigorous academic standards for student performance; (2) monitoring the performance of all schools in light of these standards and taking corrective action when appropriate; (3) administering an accountability system that informs the public how the schools and the students are performing from year to year, and releasing the names of the schools that are on the academic watch list; (4) overseeing, whether through independent boards or otherwise, establishment and implementation of standards for licenses, license renewal, and advanced certification of teachers, together with standards for preservice, induction, and ongoing professional development programs, as recommended in the 1996 Task Force Report cited in part 1; (5) setting general policies supportive of the decentralized, performance-based approach; (6) assisting school districts in implementing partnerships that will integrate preparation, induction, and professional development opportunities for teachers, again as proposed in the aforementioned Task Force Report; (7) providing an assistance function that enables, but does not require, schools to select from a list of qualified intermediate providers (independent contractors) of the kinds of services needed by schools in helping them to improve their performance; (8) providing a research and development function that helps schools to become aware of, and implement, new technologies and innovative ideas for improving their performance; and (9) overseeing the state funding of public schools.

The truth is that if the School Code were revamped along the above lines, it would probably make sense to eliminate the ISBE and create a new cabinet Secretary of Education with broad responsibility over the whole continuum of education from prekindergarten through university graduate school. A single cabinet would focus more intently on how the colleges and universities can best meet their responsibility for training able teachers for the public schools.

INCREASING THE SUPPLY OF WELL-QUALIFIED PRINCIPALS AND TEACHERS

Horace Mann was obsessed with the need to make the teaching profession more attractive to able young men and women. During his first year as the first secretary of the Massachusetts Board of Education, he noted the "extensive want of competent teachers for the common schools."[1] Mann made this observation in the 1830s, but it is true in our region today—so much so, that most of our recommendations are aimed primarily at making the positions of principal and teacher much more attractive as a long-term career to people who have a high aptitude for these careers and a deep commitment to helping students learn. That will not happen until we as a society come once again to esteem the roles of principal and teacher and hold them out to the best young students as among the worthiest of callings in life.

This cultural sea change will manifest itself in several ways. First, we will begin to pay the salaries that will attract and retain top principals and teachers. Second, we will take recruiting much more seriously. Every successful enterprise understands that its future depends on how well it recruits the next generation of top talent. The seniormost officials and every school principal in the district should be intimately involved in the task of attracting able teachers.

Third, we urge local school districts, in exercising their existing powers, to adopt performance-based bonus systems that will reward teachers in their district who who perform well beyond established goals for student performance. The performance bonus could be granted to a school on the basis of individual performance or distributed among the school's teachers in equal amounts. State funding for such bonus plans should be directed to schools in distressed neighborhoods. In addition, private-sector funds should be raised for this purpose, following New York City's example.

Fourth, we must radically upgrade the institutions that teach the teachers and eliminate superficial curricula requirements. Students spend excessive time taking required courses in educational theory; they are discouraged from pursuing interdisciplinary approaches; they are not adequately trained in the educational uses of technology; and they are subjected to the latest educational fads. The ISBE has the formal authority to make the curricula requirements more substantive and exciting for college students of ability, but it has not exercised the will to convert any but a few of the teachers colleges to this way of thinking. The pressure on teachers colleges to change will have to come primarily from school boards and the private sector.

The most outstanding private universities and colleges produce only a tiny portion of the nation's public school teachers even though many high-performing students are seeking careers in public service. All universities in the region must be urged to explore ways to heighten the interest of their students in pursuing careers as teachers at the primary and secondary school levels. This task will require the universities to take seriously the recruitment of high school students who have the potential for going to college and becoming good teachers.

Fifth, we must also develop ways of attracting well-educated people in their thirties and forties who have held jobs in business or the professions and are looking for a more satisfying, if less remunerative, career. In this regard, the 1997 amendments to the School Code are promising. We strongly urge the ISBE to establish the Alternative Route to Teacher Certification program on terms that substantially eliminate technical education course requirements and that identify high-potential candidates who need only a year or so of mentoring and seminars to develop their teaching skills.

Finally, there is a great shortage of able, well-trained principals who are adept at recruiting, motivating, and evaluating teachers; who are familiar with the educational benefits of technology; who know how to work with teachers effectively in designing curricula and improving teacher performance; and who can see to the accountability and operational aspects of the job. A principal's performance should be measured in large part on his or her power to recruit able teachers. And the identification and screening of candidates for the job of principal, whether by local school councils in Chicago or by local school districts outside the city, must be carried out in accordance with sophisticated techniques adapted in part from the business world.[2] The ISBE and the district superintendents, together with principals' associations, should take much more initiative for the professional development of principals to enable them to operate effectively in a performance-based system.

ESTABLISHING OPERATING AUTONOMY FOR SCHOOL MANAGEMENT AND PUBLIC SCHOOL CHOICE FOR PARENTS

Top-quality principals and teachers must be given responsibility for the performance of their individual schools and have wide discretion in such matters as curriculum design, the purchase and use of technology, teacher recruitment and compensation policy, and student dress and behavioral codes. The principal should have authority to require parents to enter into a compact with the school to see to their children's compliance with these code requirements.

There are corollaries to local school autonomy. One is the freedom of parents to choose to send their child to any school in the district, provided they are willing to enter into the

required compact, if any. Another is the obligation of local school management to report annually to the community on the results of the school's performance in accordance with uniform performance standards prescribed for all schools by the ISBE. Finally, district management must monitor the performance of each of its schools. In the case of an underperforming school, district management must take steps aimed at remediation. Failing remediation, the school should be placed under the control of one of the district's more successful schools. In this way, the very best principals will be given the opportunity for increased responsibility and compensation.

Of course, a system of school autonomy and parental choice along these lines will not work unless there is a much higher level of intolerance for poor teachers, as detailed below. Nor will such a system work on a widespread basis except under a tax system where parents receive portable vouchers in an amount per student that is the same across the region. In fact, the voucher amount for students requiring various levels of special education should be calibrated at rates higher than the basic rate so that schools will be encouraged to accept such students.

OVERHAULING THE SYSTEM OF TEACHER CERTIFICATION AND TENURE

The ISBE should exercise its newly granted power and authority to implement the 1997 amendments concerning teacher certification, using performance-based measures to screen out unqualified applicants for the initial four-year certificate and to prevent poorly performing teachers from obtaining the five-year Standard Teaching Certificate. The potential of these new tools for changing the current culture of "teachers for life" cannot be overestimated. The question is whether the ISBE has the will to use them as forcefully as possible.

The ISBE, in carrying out its teacher certification responsibilities, should utilize the standards developed by the Interstate New Teacher Assessment and Support Consortium, for new teachers, and by the National Board for Professional Teaching Standards, for teachers in the field. These two sets of standards represent a major breakthrough, and they have been adopted in a number of other states.[3]

TARGETING THE LOW-PERFORMING SCHOOLS

We propose a set of near-term strategies for improving student performance at the lowest-performing schools: a benchmarking system that uses updated IGAP standardized tests (aligned with revised state standards for what students are expected to learn in each grade) to measure student progress; salaries for the most outstanding teachers and principals that are competitive with those paid in the rest of the region; an incentive system, aligned with these goals, that rewards and recognizes those schools that meet the student performance goals assigned to them; a sophisticated mentoring and coaching system, using successful principals from high-performing schools, to improve the management skills of principals and the teaching and technology skills of the teachers and to help them learn from those schools that have been most effective in improving their performance; the infusion of new blood into the teaching staffs of these schools, in part by special use of the new alternative route program to bring in highly qualified and committed second-career teachers; a peer-review system and a streamlined dismissal process that will facilitate the termination of the very substantial numbers of bad teachers who undermine educational goals and demoralize the many teachers who take their jobs seriously; and finally, the greater utilization of such accountability mechanisms as probation, remediation, and restructuring. The administrators and teachers of a school threatened with being reconstituted have a powerful incentive for taking corrective measures.

In addition, our strategies aimed at strengthening neighborhoods and increasing household mobility, described in chapter 8, should further improve the prospects for equality of educational opportunity over the longer term. After all, most low-performing schools are populated chiefly with poor minority children living in marginalized neighborhoods.

ADDRESSING URGENT CAPITAL NEEDS

Over the next seven to ten years, at least $10 billion will be required to finance the renovation, construction, and equipment of school facilities in the region. Certain of our tax-reform recommendations partially address this need. In addition, there are other mechanisms to help local districts finance capital improvements—for example, the reallocation of general state aid to provide a guarantee of last resort, or the establishment by the state of a capital investment trust fund. We simply must maintain facilities, improve their accessibility for students with disabilities, and equip every school in the region with current information and communications technologies.

ENHANCING SCHOOL CHOICE

There is no single approach to solving the educational problems of large urban school systems, but the expansion of school-choice programs would inject market forces to propel the more fundamental systemic changes we seek. Among the options that should be considered and actively pursued are: liberalizing the existing charter-school legislation in Illinois; enacting an inter- and intradistrict public school–choice program consistent with the above recommendations respecting local school autonomy and parental choice within the public school system; and more choices that would include vouchers or tax credits for students who want to attend private schools. While there is still much to learn about the efficacy of such choice programs, and efforts will be required to ensure that the least advantaged are given genuine access to such options, we should move forward expeditiously to expand such alternatives. A pilot private school–choice program should be developed in the near term. Any such effort should include a strong research component to evaluate the program's effectiveness and careful assessment of the educational outcomes.

The Care and Nurture of Children

CHICAGO BUSINESS COLLABORATIVE FOR DEPENDENT CARE

Private employers should work closely with the Chicago affiliate of the national American Business Collaborative for Quality Dependent Care (ABC). The objective of this collaboration is to pool resources to increase the availability of quality child-care services in this region. Through ABC, companies in the Chicago metropolitan area can secure expert advice on how to conduct employee needs assessments and then develop strategies for dependent care. In the process, employers learn how to identify potential community vendors, whose services mirror employees' child-care needs.

STATE INITIATIVES

At the state level, incentives need to be in place to encourage child-care centers and family child-care networks to improve their quality. The state should pay a higher rate of reimbursement for services rendered to those centers and family child-care homes with NAEYC accreditation, referred to in chapter 1. As part of the licensing process for centers and family child-care homes, the state should include quality standards such as lower child-to-adult ratios, a curriculum designed to stimulate children and teach them basic skills, and avenues for parental involvement. Finally, the Illinois legislature needs to appropriate funds on an annual basis for quality enhancement and capacity building. We recommend increasing the quality/capacity-building set-aside to 10 percent of the total child-care budget, or currently about $40 million per year. This appropriation could be used to invest in facilities and training for all types of providers; develop and expand family daycare home networks; pay a higher rate to programs that are open at nontraditional hours; provide incentives to serve special-needs kids; and pay a higher rate to providers who have demonstrated excellence through accreditation. The City of Chicago's joint initiative with area foundations to invest $16 million over the next five years to improve the quality of child-care centers through the NAEYC accreditation project is laudatory.

MAKING CHILD CARE MORE AFFORDABLE

Metropolis 2020 recommends that businesses in the Chicago metropolitan region help support their employees with families through employee benefit programs. For example, Con Agra Refrigerated Foods has instituted a model program which combines partnerships with child-care centers near their plants and a pretax dependent-care assistance plan (DCAP). Con Agra makes a contribution for the startup costs of the centers and pays for a portion of the weekly cost of care for each of its employees. The employees' portion of the cost of care is deducted from their paychecks and placed in a DCAP. In addition, companies can offer temporary disability insurance and expanded parental leave to parents of newborn infants. Given the scarcity, poor quality, and relative expense of child care for infants and toddlers, paid or unpaid parental leave could offer parents an alternative to reliance on such care.

Metropolis 2020 also recommends that companies study the option of offering child-care subsidies in their menu of employee benefit options. This may enable two-parent working families to maximize their benefit-plan options. It may be less beneficial to single-parent families who will most likely need to select medical insurance as their major benefit.

The State of Illinois should ease the eligibility requirements for child-care subsidies, particularly for low-income parents who are enrolled in training programs to improve or acquire employment skills. The state should also liberalize its subsidy programs so as to enable low-income parents to buy child care with 75 percent of the providers in their communities. The cost of raising the basic rate ceiling to the 75th percentile would be approximately $100 million per year in new child-care subsidies. Higher ceilings are especially needed to afford access to licensed and accredited programs offering child care at nontraditional hours.

REDESIGNING HEALTH-CARE DELIVERY FOR POOR CHILDREN

We do not have the answer to the question of how to ensure that children from the time of conception, no matter how poor, are provided with adequate health-care services.[4] But we must find that answer if we are to realize the goals of this plan: to ensure the economic vibrancy of the region and to bring about the best possible conditions of living for all its residents. Fortunately, this region is rich in the resources and expertise required to find that answer and develop an agenda of private- and public-sector actions. To this end, we recommend that Metropolis 2020 begin by appointing a task force in consultation with other appropriate institutions.

ENHANCING THE REGION'S COMPETITIVE VIGOR

*A*ll the recommendations in part 2 are aimed directly or indirectly at strengthening the economic and social well-being of the region's residents. In this chapter we make more targeted recommendations for strengthening the economy of the region.

Improving the Region's Workforce-Development Programs

The region must consolidate and coordinate existing workforce-development programs and funding streams. No regionwide plan for workforce development currently exists, and the present array of governmental programs creates undue duplication and inefficiency, often undermining potentially useful collaboration among providers. Mayor Daley's recent decision to create a cabinet-level post, Commissioner of Workforce Development, is a step in the right direction. This commissioner will oversee the consolidated operations of two preexisting entities, the Workforce Board and the Mayor's Office of Employment and Training. This type of consolidation needs to be significantly widened to include other programs across the metropolitan region.

There is also a pressing need for universal, performance-based standards for the evaluation of education and training programs, particularly those offered by community col-

leges. These standards should pertain to placement rates, wage levels, and long-term retention results. Also, a coordinated, long-term tracking system should be developed to enable the state, county, and local government agencies and/or training vendors to document work histories, retention rates, and promotion and wages of employed and unemployed service recipients, including youths.

Coordination between business, social-service organizations, and academically oriented community colleges is also necessary to promote the relevance of training to a range of employment opportunities. In addition, training programs for new workers should take place at work, where the social and behavioral aspects of workplace participation can best be learned. Community colleges should give credit toward degrees for completion of approved on-the-job training programs.

Services to address major employment barriers other than skill deficits must be adequately funded. These include many issues addressed elsewhere in the plan such as child care, transportation, and affordable housing. Retention efforts should also be expanded and adequately funded. These include re-placement, career development, and additional post-placement support services (for example, mentoring).

Businesses should directly support workforce-development improvements by participating in and encouraging replication of successful partnerships with local nonprofit organizations and/or community colleges, such as the Chicago Manufacturing Technology "Bridge." Employers have been instrumental in designing the curriculum and identifying job placements for graduates of this innovative program, which links Richard J. Daley College, three community-based organizations, and the Illinois Institute of Technology (IIT).

Graduates of Daley College's associate degree program in manufacturing technology are placed in jobs and then enroll in IIT's bachelor of manufacturing technology program. Tuition support is provided by the employers of nearly all students in this evening and weekend program designed to prepare them for full-time employment as technical supervisors and technical salespersons.

The Chicagoland Business Partners program, recently established by the City of Chicago–Cook County Welfare Reform Task Force, offers a valuable resource to assist companies seeking to connect with relevant local organizations and to obtain guidance in establishing an effective welfare-to-work hiring process. The Partners program should be supported and expanded to serve and connect employers throughout the metropolitan region.[1]

Reforming the Cook County Classification System

At present, the Cook County classification system and the superstructure of state equalization (the state multiplier, which is 2.1 for Cook County) means that taxes on commercial and industrial properties in Cook County are about twice as high on average as they would be if those same properties were located in the collar counties. Moreover, this system (as complicated by the tradition in Cook of undervaluation) means that owners of residential properties pay much less in property taxes, on average, than do collar county owners of similarly valued residential properties.

The principal problem with this system is that it provides a perverse incentive for employers to locate commercial and industrial facilities outside of Cook. It is true that business location and relocation decisions are influenced by other important factors such as access to skilled labor and to transportation routes. Nevertheless, tax considerations can tip the balance at the margin. Ideally, employers should be able to make such decisions solely on the basis of rational business considerations and without having to react to a structural bias in the tax system such as that posed by the Cook County classification system.

Two broad tax-reform studies were completed just prior to the publication of this plan: one under the direction of James M. Houlihan, treasurer of Cook County , and the other, a Governor's Commission on Property Tax Reform, chaired by Timothy S. Bramlet, president of the Taxpayers' Federation. Metropolis 2020 should establish a task force to assess these studies and work toward solutions.

These efforts should remedy the disparity in Cook between residential and commercial taxes, resulting in reductions for commercial and industrial properties. The total net burden on most Cook County taxpayers should decline as a result of the implementation of the proposals for more equitable funding of education. If Illinois assumes a greater share of education costs, Cook County school districts will be less dependent on the property tax base to fund their operations.

Developing Intermodal Freight Centers

The following recommendations respecting freight transportation are aimed at achieving three objectives: (1) strengthening the competitive advantages available to Chicago-area businesses; (2) improving the connectivity between freight modes to increase intermodal efficiency; and (3) minimizing negative impacts of goods movement on the region's personal mobility system.

The present archaic complex of railroad yards, and the switching systems for transferring railcars, trailers, and containers between these yards, should be rationalized into a half dozen or so super intermodal centers linked by dedicated freightways in an environment separated from personal vehicles. The I-55 corridor would be a logical place to begin given the close proximity of a large number of intermodal yards and rail lines. The network could be financed in part through user fees.

It is recommended that a study be commissioned, perhaps jointly by the city, the state, and the private sector, to examine whether the intermodal freight centers could be financed by selling off excess acreage after consolidation of the rail yards, and to determine if the condemnation power of the city might be appropriately used to create some of these new freight centers.

Without detracting from the huge investments in freight operations at O'Hare, other studies should be undertaken to assess increasing air freight capacity in the region by utilizing regional airports with excess capacity, particularly the Gary site, which has access to transportation links, proximity to a region with substantial underemployment, and space for expansion of runways. A study should determine whether and to what extent the Gary site can be so exploited without conflicting with the air-space requirements of Midway. Another study should consider whether the Port of Chicago and Indiana's Burns Harbor port administration should be combined into one Chicago Port Authority in order to eliminate duplication and coordinate economic development, port investments, and intermodal facility investments.

In the meantime, we recommend that three near-term strategies be pursued. First, top priority should be given to the City of Chicago (where most of the switching yards are located) for upgrading connections between intermodal hubs, air freight centers, port facilities, and other major freight facilities and the interstate highways, including elimination of low-clearance obstructions and improvement of turning capabilities at key intersections. Prioritization of projects should be established under the CATS funding process.

Second, the appropriate governmental units should reduce the number of highway/rail grade crossings in the region and improve the remaining crossings across the region to improve safety, expedite train movements, and reduce traffic congestion.

Third, increased fees on truck and rail movements should provide most of the wherewithal for building dedicated truckways and otherwise easing the movement of rail and truck traffic. These measures would at the same time improve car and bus mobility.

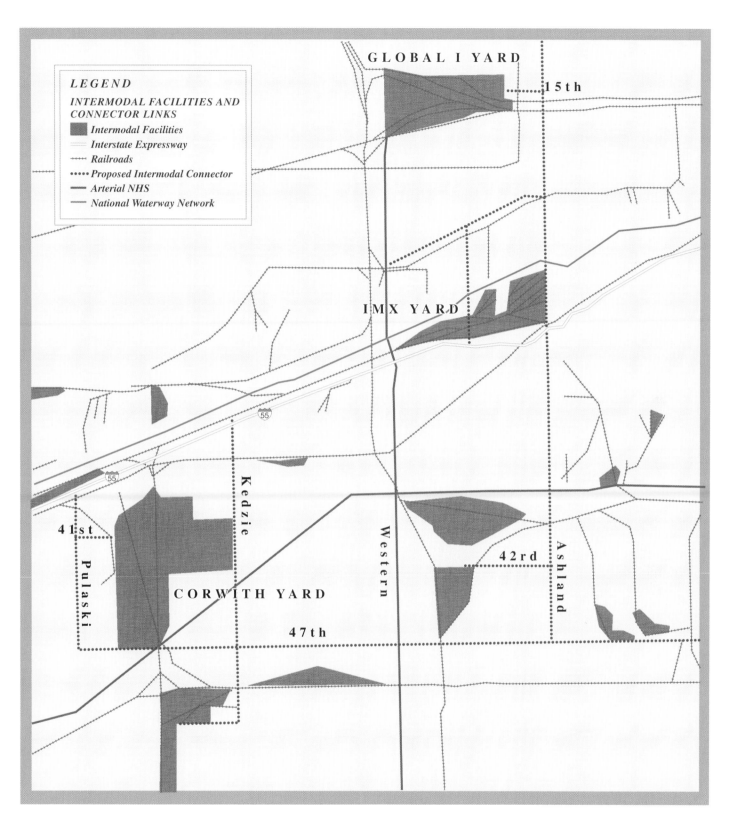

LEGEND

INTERMODAL FACILITIES AND
CONNECTOR LINKS

- Intermodal Facilities
- Interstate Expressway
- Railroads
- Proposed Intermodal Connector
- Arterial NHS
- National Waterway Network

GLOBAL I YARD

15th

IMX YARD

55

55

Kedzie

41st

Pulaski

Western

42rd

Ashland

CORWITH YARD

47th

Map depicting intermodal facilities in a portion of south Chicago. Intermodal connectors link major passenger and freight facilities to the National Highway System.

Fourth, a central control and monitoring facility is needed for all rail activity (both commuter and freight) in the Chicago Terminal District. At present all railroads do their own monitoring with very little advance communication and planning, and the result is unexpected, lengthy delays at track crossovers.

Improving Air Transportation

EXPAND CAPACITY AT O'HARE

If the Chicago region is to reach its potential as an air transportation center, O'Hare's aviation capacity must grow significantly and in a manner consistent with all safety requirements. We must therefore begin immediately either the construction of an additional runway or the reconfiguration of the existing runways to provide for more runways in parallel than in the existing configuration. This additional capacity is needed if our region is to maintain its preeminence as a domestic hub and realize its potential as an international gateway.

SUPPORT GENERAL AVIATION

The planned closing of Meigs Field in 2001 demands an immediate data-based evaluation of Chicago's future general aviation needs and a comprehensive study to determine where the growing volume will be accommodated in the next two decades given the city's planned

elimination of 14,000 general aviation operations from Midway and O'Hare and the need to relocate 50,000 operations from Meigs. A state-of-the-art downtown heliport should be constructed (possible sites include the top of the old post office, the Jardine filtration plant, and Meigs Field), and its impact on the volume of fixed-wing business flights then should be built into the volume model and forecasts for general aviation.

LAND BANKING FOR THIRD AIRPORT

Although there is wide variability among state, federal, and City of Chicago aviation-demand projections, all of the forecasts support the need for a significant increase in point-to-point air capacity over the next twenty years. Land banking through options or purchase for a third airport at Peotone should proceed so as to facilitate transportation planning for the next twenty to thirty years. While reviewing the feasibility of Peotone as the site for future point-to-point airport capacity in Chicago may be beneficial, allowing the State of Illinois to preserve future flexibility is justified. No passenger facility or other O'Hare revenues should be used for this purpose and construction should not begin until needed. Further, it is important to understand that capacity added to Midway or a third airport cannot be a substitute for required capacity at O'Hare.

COMMON PLANNING DATA

It is essential that the State of Illinois and City of Chicago reach consensus over basic aviation issues such as forecasts of future demand and required capacity at Chicago metropolitan area airports. They should use NIPC data to reach a consensus on future airport capacity requirements. If the state and city cannot reach agreement, then NIPC should develop forecasts of future airport-capacity needs which set priorities for capital projects involving changes in regional airport capacity.

Assessing the Viability of High-Speed Rail

The Chicago Metropolis 2020 Council should establish a task force to evaluate the studies of high-speed rail completed to date and to assess (1) the levels of ridership and revenues that would be required to yield an adequate return on capital investment, (2) the market demand for this service, and (3) the indirect economic and social benefits, if any, in reducing short-haul air traffic and providing easy connections between the city centers of the metropolitan regions in the system. Based on that assessment, the task force would determine whether to support efforts to secure the necessary federal funding and encourage the prompt development of such a network. The task force should weigh heavily the impact of any high-speed rail proposal on Midway Airport and its continued importance as a major anchor to the economic well-being of the surrounding area.

Streamlining the Property-Assessment System

To solve the administration problem described in chapter 4, we propose that a nonelected, professional office of assessor be created within each county. The office of township assessor would be eliminated, and each county would be responsible for the valuation process for its territory. The six counties would then be in a position, as a next step, to enter into an intergovernmental agreement to centralize certain professional support staff functions and mechanisms, including a mechanism for publicly disclosing property tax valuations. This agreement should also contain provisions for the certification and recertification of county assessors on a professional basis. This recommendation should be implemented independently of all other recommendations relating to tax reform.

Preparing the Center City for Its New Role and Restoring the Competitiveness of the Inner City

The decentralization of manufacturing activity in the region is well understood. But an important trend of growth in the service sectors in the central business district of Chicago and other high-density centers in the region is often overlooked by the focus on the loss of manufacturing jobs in the region. True, the portion of private-sector jobs in manufacturing in the region declined from 45 to 18 percent from 1963 to 1998, but the portion of such jobs in services grew from 11 percent to 36 percent. As Michael Porter argues,[2] in services, proximity is much more important than in manufacturing. He points to certain center-city clusters that are among the most rapidly growing part of the economy: entertainment and tourism; education and knowledge creation; health services and health technology; financial services; business-related services; media and publishing; logistics and transportation.

STRATEGIES FOR ENHANCING THE REGION AS A HIGH-TECHNOLOGY CENTER

Among all economic regions in the United States, the Chicago area currently ranks fourth in high-technology employment, ahead of Boston, Seattle, and Research Triangle Park.

The region's seven largest technology-intensive sectors are telecommunications, life science, electronics, computer software, information technology and services, advanced materials, and environmental technologies. The region's strength in these areas is owing largely to the region's pool of highly skilled talent and a vital research and development infrastructure, two of the key elements for supporting technology-based economic development. But there are other areas that must be addressed if our region is to become a top high-technology center, including (1) the need for an adequate supply of capital for all stages of growth, particularly the early stages; and (2) an effective marketing program that communicates the region's strengths and the need for public-/private-sector coalitions to ensure that our region is responding appropriately to the unfolding implications of the Internet, wireless communications, and other information and communication technologies that will have a profound effect on the ways in which we live and work and engage in economic transactions.

There are now under way a number of initiatives that respond to some of these needs. First, the City of Chicago is establishing an incubator/support facility for startup firms in the software sector. This facility will entail an information technology center. Second, the Illinois Coalition[3] is proposing the development of a venture fund that would supply seed capital to early-stage technology companies in the region to fund the continued expansion of the technology businesses, helping them create jobs. The Illinois Coalition plans to market the state and the region as an important center of science and technology and to compete more effectively with regions that have been far more aggressive in communicating their attractiveness to technology companies. Metropolis 2020 enthusiastically endorses this effort.

An organized effort is needed to persuade scientifically and technically trained graduates of the region's universities to look for employment in the region. This effort should include regular visits by employers to college campuses to engage the students well before they enter the labor market, internship programs with firms in the region, job fairs, and seminars and conferences that show off the region's strengths and its attractiveness as a high-technology community with world-renowned centers for research.

INDUSTRIAL REDEVELOPMENT STRATEGIES

Industrial users in Chicago face many obstacles, but the city's central location also offers industry some key advantages: abundance of labor; areas with excellent access to highways and intermodal rail/truck facilities; mass-transit access; and proximity to an expanding, dynamic downtown that is creating a growing need for a wide range of support services traditionally found in the city's industrial districts, including warehousing distribution, construction, maintenance-related businesses, and telecommunications services.

In recent years, the city has intensified its efforts to promote industrial growth by upgrading the physical environment of industrial areas and assembling land for use as industrial parks.[4] We strongly endorse this strategy and encourage the city to proceed with its plans for creating several new industrial corridors.

An indispensable tool in pursuing this strategy is tax increment financing (TIF), which was enacted into law in Illinois in 1977. TIF bonds are used to pay for infrastructure improvements and for the acquisition and preparation of land for redevelopment, to pay back loans from the City of Chicago's Brownfields Program for environmental remediation, and to pay for job training and related educational programs, and for measures needed to attract or retain a specific industrial user.

At present there are 242 TIF districts in the region, of which 47 are in the City of Chicago. The city estimates that TIF projects have created approximately 9,500 new jobs and saved approximately 25,000 others. Twenty-eight percent of the newly created jobs and 27 percent of the retained jobs involved industrial businesses.[5] One of the most serious obstacles the city faces in carrying out the long and complex process of assembling industrial corridors is posed by a flawed property tax system that undertaxes vacant land (or land with abandoned buildings), thereby encouraging private landowners to play a waiting game in the sale and development of real estate for their property. To remedy this situation, we recommend that the Illinois legislature reform the property tax system so as to give municipalities the authority to levy a limited supplemental tax if a property that clearly has strong potential is not being developed.

INITIATIVES FOR ENHANCING THE COMPETITIVENESS OF THE INNER CITY

Metropolis 2020 was created to implement the recommendations set forth in this report. That organization, which is composed of key leaders throughout the region, is described in the last chapter. One of the task forces to be established by Metropolis 2020 will devote its efforts, in conjunction with other organizations, to implementing initiatives for enhancing the competitiveness of the more distressed neighborhoods of the City of Chicago.

Residents of these neighborhoods are the most economically disadvantaged across all socioeconomic indicators. Representing nearly half of the city's population (19 percent of the region's population), their unemployment rates are more than two-and-a-half times higher than for the region, likewise for the percentage of people living below poverty. More than 40 percent of adults in these neighborhoods are without a high school education. Given these statistics, it is clear that specific strategies to improve the economic viability of these neighborhoods are necessary. As many studies have shown, the economic health of the region and that of the urban core are intricately linked. Moreover, these neighborhoods, located to the west and south of the central business district, exhibit a number of competitive advantages as business locations.

A recent study of businesses in Chicago's distressed neighborhoods identified a number of strategies for growth in four business clusters—strategies that would create employment for the local residents. These included (1) *manufacturing:* retaining existing businesses by proactively addressing company expansion issues, expanding site availability, and increasing cost competitiveness vis-à-vis the suburbs; (2) *commercial services:* positioning inner-city companies to provide outsourced services to professional and business services firms as well as the tourism and convention businesses located in the Loop; (3) *retail:* meeting the estimated $1.5 billion unmet demand for retail goods and services in these neighborhoods; and (4) *transportation:* improving the competitive position of the Port of Chicago and developing employer-driven training programs for the region's intermodal truck/rail centers, which are already experiencing a shortage of qualified workers.[6]

CREATING A CENTRALIZED DATABASE AND FASHIONING A COMPETITIVE STRATEGY FOR THE TWENTY-FIRST CENTURY

In 1997, the Civic Committee of the Commercial Club and the Chicagoland Chamber of Commerce formed, and have since funded, a new nonprofit organization, "World Business Chicago" (WBC). Since then, WBC's task has been to create a sophisticated economic database for metropolitan Chicago (on an expanded nine-county basis). The data has been built up from local sources to encompass meaningful information on the entire region. It is being augmented by other relevant data sources throughout the region as well as pertinent external sources. The plan is to assemble data necessary to evaluate individual sub-areas as well as the entire region. The database will also contain economic information on metropolitan areas with which we compete for investment. The results of this effort are being placed on a Web site, and all the data will be made available to public and private organizations at no charge.

This database should be the starting point for developing a competitive strategy for the twenty-first century. What is needed is a comprehensive, strategic study of the region's economy and industry clusters that would identify the region's strengths, weaknesses, opportunities, and threats in a systematic format. Such an undertaking would include a competitive analysis of what other metropolitan regions are doing to improve their economic development prospects, and the efficacy of the Chicago region's efforts in comparison. Moreover, such a study would identify the special needs and opportunities that exist in specific industry groups that are critical to the region's growth prospects.

As the information system is further refined, it should go beyond economic and demographic information and inform fledgling entrepreneurs precisely which organizations provide what kinds of services. Small and medium-sized businesses usually do not have the resources to acquire this type of information on their own. This type of database should highlight innovative programs. For example, programs in the education and training areas might help employers meet their workforce needs. Small businesses are often unfamiliar with existing workforce-training programs. This information gap is particularly critical given that small and medium-sized businesses are often the best employment prospects for entry-level workers.

At present there are more than seventy economic development organizations in the region. Many of them work in ignorance of one another's actions and objectives. One of the earliest tasks of WBC has been to coordinate the activities of the various economic-development agencies in the region, creating the mutual trust and confidence required to build a unified database and a coordinated marketing program. WBC now has a regional advisory committee comprised of representatives of these agencies and organizations. This committee provides a direct communications link between these agencies and the planning, programs, and initiatives of WBC. In addition, these coordinating efforts are being pursued by such other organizations as the Chicago Partnership for Economic Development and the Chicagoland Chamber of Commerce.

POSITIONING THE REGION AS A CENTER FOR ENTREPRENEURSHIP

Entrepreneurship is critical to the continued vibrancy of the region. Entrepreneurial companies are a principal source of future growth. Therefore, it is imperative to effectively position the region as a center for entrepreneurs.

A number of studies of entrepreneurship have been conducted over the last several years. The key findings of these studies are as follows:

➤ New enterprise development usually occurs within regional industrial clusters, partly because each cluster has particular locational advantages.

➤ Many cities and states have aggressive programs and strategies for enhancing the growth of new business.

➤ Fourteen of the top twenty entrepreneurial hot spots are in regions west of the Mississippi River. The Rocky Mountain area is especially rich in entrepreneurial enterprises. Our region, which is not on the list of the top twenty, is rated about average in terms of its attractiveness to entrepreneurs. Although the diversity of its economy is regarded as an overall strength, finding educated workers here remains a problem.

There are five key components of a good support environment for entrepreneurship: capital access, technology transfer, skills development, a support network, and communications. Fortunately, the six-county area possesses portions of each of these fundamental characteristics.

In respect to access to equity capital, it is widely perceived that high-growth and high-technology startups find it difficult to get seed and early-stage capital, and information on sources of such capital is not readily available. Accordingly, we recommend the establishment of a facilitation office, funded through a private/public partnership. One of its roles would be to provide a value-added matching service between entrepreneurs and sources of early-stage capital appropriate to their business requirements. Also, industry groups should push for the expansion of existing matching programs in the technology and manufacturing areas and create additional programs to target the region's other clusters.

Universities in this region have not done as good a job of exploiting technology transfer opportunities as other world-class educational institutions.[7] It is recommended that a forum be organized to bring academics/administrators from universities with nationally recognized technology transfer programs together with their counterparts at universities in this region. Further, each local university should develop a technology transfer blueprint. These programs will be successful only with the support of the president, the university's board, and the passionate commitment of a faculty champion.

In the matter of skills development, innovative features of university entrepreneurship programs elsewhere in the nation (for example, student competitions that provide networking opportunities, and coordination of seed capital for qualified student ventures) have not been adequately adopted by universities and colleges in our region. We urge our local universities and colleges to benchmark themselves against world-class entrepreneurial curricula at other universities and seek to improve their programs accordingly. We believe that community colleges are ideally suited to reach into the entrepreneurial community and provide practical, hands-on skills development for operators of small businesses. The facilitation office recommended above should ensure that the new programs are well publicized.

At present, the entrepreneurial network in the region is quite limited, and the proposed entrepreneurial facilitation office should take a leadership role in improving networking opportunities, outreach, and accessibility, and forging linkages with existing network organizations such as the Chicagoland Chamber of Commerce.

There is a strong need for a greater communications focus on the region's unique characteristics as a major urban center that is supportive of the needs of entrepreneurs. The proposed facilitation office should have a public-relations arm, responsible for channeling to the media relevant stories on entrepreneurial success and the importance of entrepreneurial activity to the region.

MARKETING THE CHICAGO REGION AS A PLACE IN WHICH TO LIVE AND WORK

The region needs to be much more aggressive and unified in promoting and marketing its considerable advantages, both internally and externally. This marketing effort needs to make certain that the region is always on the short list as a desirable place to run and operate a business and as a place to live.

For two years running, Chicago has been the top major metropolitan area in the United States in this regard, although on a relative basis (i.e., based on population size), some smaller cities have outperformed Chicago.

The region has a number of key attractions, as described in the introduction. Metropolitan Chicago is an attractive location where young professionals want to work and live. Both to keep our best young people here and to attract others who will drive our economic growth in the future, we must improve on that attractiveness. The secret to doing so lies in developing toward a community of the whole rather than remaining the preserve of isolated communities.

Over the last year, WBC has embarked on an aggressive effort to attract global companies to this region. It began by conducting a comprehensive review of economic-development marketing efforts in other domestic locations as well as in London, Singapore, Tokyo, Frankfurt, and other international cities. WBC identifies target companies using peer-to-peer contacts and a wide variety of other sources. It then communicates with these companies using letters of introduction from business leaders, arranging trade missions and marketing trips, employing telemarketing techniques, and publishing brochures, articles, and speeches.

WBC's principal brochure contains a fact book with detailed statistics concerning the region. It has been translated into Japanese and will be translated into other languages as appropriate. Each of the nine counties in the expanded metropolitan area is in the process of preparing an insert on itself for inclusion in the brochure. Metropolis 2020 should establish a continuing task force to assess the progress of WBC and determine whether to recommend additional marketing efforts to supplement those of WBC in niche areas.

GOVERNING THE REGION

*T*his chapter presents two recommendations respecting the governance of the region: the creation of a new regional coordinating mechanism for enabling and encouraging the myriad of general-purpose governments in the region to think and act as a region in respect to critical regional issues; and the establishment of a task force to conduct a study and make recommendations for the streamlining of government in the region, with emphasis on reducing the number of special districts.

A Regional Coordinating Council

One of the most important recommendations in this plan is the proposal for a regional coordinating mechanism that can deal effectively with the interrelationships among policies and practices concerning transportation, land use, housing, and the environment. Without such a mechanism, we cannot go very far in meeting the challenges described in part 1.

The State of Illinois is the source of substantially all regional and local planning and regulatory functions pertaining to land use and the environment. As a practical matter, given its financial role, it also controls all significant transportation planning functions in the region. Because northeastern Illinois contains over two-thirds of the state's entire population, the issues that are significant to this region are important to the state as a whole. Yet the State of Illinois has not addressed these regional concerns in any systematic or comprehensive fashion. Absent from the vast array of state policies and programs affecting the four areas of transportation, land use, housing, and the environment is a framework that strongly motivates counties and municipalities within the region to correlate their local goals with the larger public interest of the region and to do so in a manner that recognizes the interrelationships among these four areas.

THE ENABLING LEGISLATION

The proposal that follows would fill this gap, utilizing an incentive-based approach. We considered and rejected the alternative "command-and-control" approach of a regional growth boundary or a regional authority to regulate municipal annexations. We believe that this more drastic approach, while successful in other parts of the United States, would not be appropriate for this region. The proposed statutory framework would reward local governments for exercising their land-use powers in a regionally coordinated manner, oriented toward common goals.

Specifically, we recommend that the State of Illinois establish a Regional Coordinating Council (RCC). The statute would begin with certain findings: that the region is confronted with increasing social and economic polarization; that uncoordinated growth, together with a lack of common goals respecting conservation and the wise use of land, pose a threat to the environment, sustainable economic development, and the health, safety, and high quality of life enjoyed by residents of the larger region; that transportation and land-use planning need to be much more closely integrated; and that it is in the public interest to experiment with pilot projects that price motor vehicles and their use in ways that will more nearly reflect the true costs of this form of travel and that could ultimately raise revenues for improving public transportation and making it a more attractive alternative or supplement to private vehicle travel.

The statute would set forth the following goals, which would define the mission of the RCC:

➤ To bring about efficient multimodal transportation systems.
➤ To encourage the availability of housing for all economic segments of the population in all parts of the region.
➤ To moderate disparities in fiscal capacity and service quality among the municipalities in the region.
➤ To encourage redevelopment in older urban areas that merit reinvestment; encourage conservation development and the retention and enjoyment of open space and agricultural lands, natural habitat, and parks.
➤ And to encourage the preservation of lands, sites, and structures that have historical significance.

The key idea behind the proposal for the RCC is that it will provide strong incentives to counties and municipalities to use their powers in ways that advance the RCC's mission. The chief incentive mechanism will be the RCC's bond-issuing function. In addition, the RCC will have other powers and responsibilities to be exercised on its own initiative to advance its mission and address critical regional issues that cannot otherwise be addressed.

THE INCENTIVE PROGRAM

Bonds would be issued by the RCC only upon its approval of an application by one or more counties and/or municipalities pertaining to newly expanding portions of the region, urbanized areas which are economically distressed, or possibly the creation of an intermodal center at a train station. Bond proceeds could be used for the building or rehabilitation of various components of the infrastructure such as highways, parking, and sanitary or stormwater sewers; for the preservation of open space; and for land purchase.

To qualify for RCC bond financing, applicants would be required to have in force local zoning ordinances and building codes that are consistent with state standards as they pertain to the adequate provision of housing opportunities; adequate local regulations in effect with reference to water resource management; an effective and vigorously enforced fair housing ordinance; and a comprehensive plan, periodically updated, that addresses the RCC's mission and that is consistent with NIPC 2020 forecasts as periodically updated by the new RCC.[1] These realistic projections of population growth would help to constrain overly ambitious planning in developing areas.

The statute would require the RCC to establish a mechanism for public participation and hearings in order to generate public understanding of the RCC's mission as it is given specificity in the RCC's strategic plan.

The RCC would seek to reinforce and accelerate the already evolving practice of intergovernmental planning for land use, transportation, and development standards in the region. The RCC would encourage municipal and county governments to enter into joint planning agreements by offering a variety of grants and other benefits in return for planning and corresponding actions.

Counties that adopt state-qualified plans could expect all agencies of state government to recognize, and avoid conflict with, such plans in the course of performing their normal functions.

Under the new framework, the RCC would actively encourage counties and municipalities to negotiate intergovernmental land-use agreements. Counties and municipalities entering such agreements would gain similar assurances of "no conflict" with future state agency actions. The state would utilize the services of the RCC as facilitator of intermunicipal agreements.

In order to reinforce the legal framework for the intergovernmental agreements called for above, this new statutory framework would clarify and reinforce the authority of local governments to enter into such agreements. A serious barrier to such cooperative agreements would be removed by implementation of the tax reforms recommended elsewhere in this document.

OTHER POWERS AND RESPONSIBILITIES OF THE RCC

In addition to the incentive program outlined above, the RCC would (1) be responsible for developing and periodically revising a long-term strategic plan for the region respecting transportation, land use, housing, wastewater services, storm water management, and water supply, and such other matters as it may deem appropriate in order to give specificity to the RCC's mission; (2) have power, in connection with new developments, to deny access to sewer systems and wastewater treatment facilities, but only where such access would have a substantial, adverse regional impact; (3) have discretion, within specified limits, to require the regional registration of vehicles and to adopt and implement pilot projects for pricing motor-vehicle travel (and parking) in high-density areas so that vehicle users more nearly pay the true costs of this form of mobility and so as to begin to raise a new source of revenue for improving public transit; and (4) receive and distribute revenues to be used to moderate disparities in fiscal capacity between the richest and poorest municipalities in the region. The vast middle, say 80 percent of the cities and villages, would be unaffected by this last function.

FUNDING THE RCC

This document is intended as a strategic guide, not as a detailed blueprint. Accordingly it does not quantify the funding needs of the RCC. It does consider a number of possible funding approaches. One possibility is a new statewide sales tax on a carefully defined category of personal services. It does not make much sense to tax a pair of shoes but not a haircut. The state would retain a small portion to cover its administrative costs. The bulk of the revenues, to the extent generated in the six-county region, would be distributed to the RCC. The tax rate would depend in part on whether it is designed as part of an overall scheme to reduce the sales tax rate on goods.

A second possible source of funding for the programs outlined above could be derived from a new state-adopted "shared sales tax system," applicable only to the region. Under such a system, the amount returned to any one municipality would not exceed in any year a specified sum, say $200 per resident, plus 50 percent of any receipts over that amount, thereby preserving an important incentive to pursue local economic development. The other 50 percent of the excess, if any, would go to the regional council to be used for funding its programs. Thus, for example, if a municipality received $1,200 per capita under the present system, it would only receive $700 under the new system. The other $500 would go into the regional pool for funding the programs of the council. In order to develop a definitive proposal, it will be necessary to prepare forecasts of revenue needs and to model the tax formula on different assumptions as to base and level of sharing.

Such a proposal could be phased in over a period of years to enable the high-sales-tax-base municipalities to shift more gradually to other forms of taxation. The proposal would not touch any supplemental sales taxes levied and collected directly by a particular community in excess of the 1 percent it receives from the state. A portion of the revenues raised by these two proposals would be distributed by the RCC in such a manner as to ensure that the total per capita sales tax revenues of every municipality in the region (including its receipts from the state) met a specified floor. The bulk (the remainder) of the revenues from these two measures would be used to service bonds issued by the RCC.

As noted in chapter 2, the unmet capital and operating needs of the region's road system and its public transportation system are immense. It will require about $500 million per year over the next decade to meet the most serious of these needs, and priority should be given to public transportation.

One possible source of funding would be an increase in auto-related taxes and license fees, to be used only for public transportation. As a first step, the state might increase its annual license fees for vehicles in the six-county region by an average of $50 per vehicle. The license fee for any particular vehicle might range from $25 to $125 as determined by a formula based on original cost and current age of the vehicle. Assuming a vehicle population in the region of 5 million or more, that would produce a total of at least $250 million per year. These funds would be transferred in trust to the RCC to be used for public transportation improvements. In addition, the RCC might be given discretion, within specified limits, to adopt and implement pilot projects for pricing motor-vehicle travel (and parking) so that vehicle users more nearly pay the true costs of this form of mobility. While the revenues raised through these experiments would be rather minimal in the early years, they could become substantial over time. Again the funds would be used solely to improve public transportation and meet operating needs.

As in the case of the other funding possibilities put forth in this section, before definitive legislative proposals can be formulated, it will be necessary to prepare projections of RCC's revenue needs and of the revenue-raising potential of different variations on our proposals.

THE GOVERNANCE OF THE RCC

The RCC should be headed by a board of trustees not to exceed fifteen in number. The board would appoint a president and chief executive officer who would serve at the pleasure of the board. We have considered a number of alternative ways in which the members of the board might be elected or appointed. Four criteria were used to assess these alternatives. First, which alternative will best ensure that the board is composed of highly competent people of integrity and good judgment? Second, which alternative will best ensure that the trustees are held accountable for their performance? Third, which will best build a sense of the common good for the region and a sense of the interdependency of its parts, both among elected local officials and among the public at large? And fourth, which will best assure that local governments play a critical role in selecting the board members? Given the RCC's lack of power to compel, and its reliance on the power to persuade, some direct connection between the RCC and the localities may be crucial to the RCC's effectiveness.

None of the alternatives is without flaws. If the trustees are elected directly by the region's voters, it is likely that many able persons will be deterred by the costs of running for office. Further, the voters are already deluged at election time with a complexity of choices for numerous offices; another set of decisions would only add to the confusion. This latter defect could be alleviated by introducing an aldermanic system, but that would not satisfy the third criterion of building a sense of the common good of the whole region.

Under another alternative, all trustees would be appointed by the governor, the mayor of Chicago, and the six county boards. The difficulty with this alternative is the question of accountability, since trustees might have allegiances to their respective political entities that override the regional interest.

A third alternative, the one we recommend, would be a confederation approach, giving votes to each of the 270 municipalities in accordance with their relative populations and to the six counties in accordance with the populations of their unincorporated areas. An appointed blue-ribbon nominating commission would select 45 candidates for the 15 offices, taking into account the distribution of the population across the region.

Governance is an art, and the devil is in the details. Should there be a blue-ribbon nominating commission, perhaps appointed by the governor? Should the chairman of the board be an appointee of the governor? Is cumulative voting desirable? How do we ensure that there is fair geographic representation? These and many other questions will need to be addressed in the process of designing a definitive proposal.

It could take years of vigorous effort to bring about the establishment of the RCC as proposed. As a first step toward this ultimate objective, we recommend moving immediately toward a consolidation of CATS and NIPC and transferring to the new planning agency all the planning functions of the RTA. The consolidated agency's first mission would be to prepare a strategic regional-transportation and land-use vision. The vision should begin with a consideration of the vision offered in this plan. Further inputs would be provided by the current effort of NIPC to develop a new regional growth strategy and by a consortium of civic and environmental organizations, including NIPC. With regard to transportation, the new strategic vision would address the key issues: the proper balance between expenditures on highway improvements and those for public transportation; the appropriate level of transportation expenditures in support of exurban expansion versus expenditures required to support city and suburban infill and redevelopment; and means of funding.

The agency's scope of planning authority should cover all areas currently within the jurisdiction of CATS, NIPC, and the RTA, and it should bring a much more intense focus on the interconnections between transportation and land-use planning. After it develops its initial vision for the region, it would turn its attention to preparing the successor to the 2020 Regional Transportation Plan, based on that new vision. The agency would be federally designated as the Metropolitan Planning Organization for this region and thus charged with maintaining the region's short-range transportation improvement program and identifying those capital projects that are to receive priority federal funding. Also, the agency would be responsible for allocating, on the basis of published criteria, the new transportation revenues identified in chapter 2. The agency would have authority to initiate capital improvement projects of strategic importance to the region as well as to approve toll highway expansions within the six-county area. Eventually, it would be assigned responsibility for airport planning and the planning and coordination of freight movement within the region.

Neither NIPC's nor CATS' functions are adequately funded at this time. Funding for the new agency should be set at a level that eliminates the need to seek voluntary contributions. There are a number of models nationally which could work well. Some metropolitan agencies are funded in part by state appropriations. Others have been assigned a small proportion of one or more regional tax levies. Still others receive revenue through a legislated local contribution formula.

This proposed agency would assure closer contact and cooperation among those at both the state and local levels now responsible for separate but overlapping planning, spending, and regulatory functions. Likewise, the new agency would generate cross-fertilization of thinking among several related professions (for example, highway engineers and environmental planners) and a greater sharing of the research information and analytical technologies now housed in separate agencies. In this way, the planning agency would prepare the way for the full-blown proposal of the new RCC described above.

Streamlining Local Government

Effective and efficient government in the region is undermined by a system of 1,246 local governments, many of which continue to exist because reform efforts are ignored by the public and resisted by officeholders whose jobs would be threatened by any streamlining effort. Metropolis 2020 intends to appoint a task force that combines members having astute political sensitivities with members from the business community who have a sharp nose for cost control and corporate simplification.

Such a task force would design strategies for implementation of the new reforms over a period of several years so as to minimize the motivation of current officeholders to try to defeat the reforms. The major aim of this study should be to substantially reduce the number of special districts in the region. There are now 558 of these single-purpose governments, such as fire-protection districts, mosquito-abatement districts, library districts, sanitary districts, and so forth. The task force should weigh various alternatives, including consolidations, eliminating some of them and either outsourcing their functions to the private sector or transferring their functions to general-purpose governments (counties, townships, or municipalities), or some combination of the above. There are extraordinary opportunities for savings—for example, the closer collaboration and sharing of resources with respect to fire, police, and correctional services, including equipment, information technologies, personnel, and facilities; and the regionalization of such functions as long-range planning for and operation of juvenile and adult detention facilities.

ADDRESSING THE PROBLEMS OF RACE AND POVERTY

C hapters 6 and 7 present, among other things, recommendations for meeting the educational and employment needs of the less-advantaged residents of the region. This chapter focuses on their special needs in the areas of housing, neighborhoods, and mobility.

Improving Housing Conditions for Poor Minorities

The following strategies are aimed at (1) creating greater opportunities for low-income households to live in mixed-income developments, and (2) affording them much greater freedom to choose to live in communities outside the poverty-concentrated areas in which so many of them now seem destined to exist. The first proposal is for strategies (supply-side strategies) that focus on the redevelopment and modernization of public housing and that encourage public-private partnerships to develop and manage new subsidized units. Second, there is a need for strategies (demand-side strategies) that concentrate on enlarging the geographic choices of poor households through vouchers and counseling. Neither set of strategies, by itself, is likely to effectively address the challenges of housing the urban poor; both are required for meaningful progress.

SUPPLY-SIDE STRATEGIES

The strategy here is to destroy the existing stock of high-rise public housing, move to a new era of mixed-income and mixed-use developments, and put an end to the terrible physical isolation of poor African Americans. Metropolis 2020 urges the CHA to proceed expeditiously with the three interim models that it has concluded will be most effective in improving the quality of life of the residents. The Cabrini-Green model will lease a certain percentage of the newly developed units in the prime Near North location for sublease to tenants who are displaced by the planned demolition of one-third of the buildings. The Henry Horner model scatters public housing units across the Westhaven neighborhood, where 50 percent of the households have one member who holds a full-time job, earning 50 to 80 percent of the median household income for the region. The other half of the Westhaven residents are very low-income families. The Robert Taylor model is a plan to create an industrial park to improve economic conditions of residents while carrying out a ten-year project to demolish the twenty-eight identical sixteen-story buildings, a project that should be accelerated to allow its residents to be relocated as quickly as possible to other public housing units or given vouchers for private-market rental units.

The federal government will have to carry out its commitment to see the Chicago Housing Authority into this new era. Accordingly, the CHA should close roughly 1,500 units per year over the next ten years. Because the market will not absorb all the families with vouchers, the CHA should secure at least 400 additional units per year on average over the next several years. This will require annual funding of roughly $40 to $50 million. Relocation assistance, job training, and counseling are essential for the 11,000 families who will have to move over the next few years. The CHA's experience, under the Section 8 program, shows that participants are more likely to make significant relocations after they have been in the training and counseling program for a year. The cost of such a program will be about $2.6 million per year. This cost includes counseling, incentive payments (for example, paying security deposits for families willing to move to less concentrated neighborhoods), and assistance in closing old utility accounts. The CHA should demolish that half of the family housing stock that has been determined to be uninhabitable and inappropriate for rehabilitation. The CHA has the funds for demolition, but only if the federal government absorbs the costs of keeping the buildings in habitable condition while they await demolition. The CHA must continue to receive the present annual grant of $120 million to cover the capital and security costs for the 40,000 units owned by it.

DEMAND-SIDE STRATEGIES: IMPROVING HOUSEHOLD MOBILITY

Demand-side strategies focus on empowering project residents to make housing choices that will improve their circumstances. The current trend of economic development has not produced many employment opportunities in the inner city. Rather, the evidence to date is that only public or publicly financed facilities are located there on any significant scale.

Anthony Downs observes that it "is access to private sector jobs, facilities, and opportunities, not public facilities, that is crucial for rejuvenating the lives of inner-city residents. Inner-city residents must also be exposed to environments that are not dominated by extreme poverty and its attendant conditions. That means sending their children to schools where most students are from working-class or middle-class homes. It means giving them job opportunities in businesses where most other workers have enough skills to earn decent incomes. It means giving them the chance to live in neighborhoods not dominated by juvenile gangs, drugs, and fear of violence. Only these can constitute real opportunities."[1]

That is the lesson of Chicago's Gautreaux Program, which began with a 1976 federal court order that forced the Department of Housing and Urban Development to use Section 8 certificates and vouchers to assist 300 to 400 public housing families a year to rent apartments in the private market throughout the metropolitan area, both in Chicago and suburban neighborhoods, in census tracts with black populations of less than thirty percent. Two decades and five thousand families later it is clear that Gautreaux families who move to suburbs where there is much greater economic diversity do better than Gautreaux families who stay in Chicago.

Section 8 certificates and vouchers supplement the difference between the household's ability to pay and the market rent. As noted earlier, the CHA currently administers more than 15,000 units under such vouchers. It anticipates an increase over the next year in the certificate and voucher pool administered by it to 19,700 households. In the past, the CHA has been able, on average, to place 1,000 households a year in the private market.

Metropolis 2020 recommends that the federal government expand the existing Section 8 certificate and voucher programs in this region, provided that the state first takes appropriate action (1) to provide the level of counseling, training, accountability, and technical assistance that is required to accommodate the enhanced voucher funding; and (2) to require every locality in the region to comply with uniform building code and zoning requirements that would open the way for the construction of substantially more rental housing and thereby encourage housing choices in stable communities with access to jobs, transportation, and other services.

Building Strong Neighborhoods

THE LOW-INCOME HOUSING TAX CREDIT

The Low-Income Housing Tax Credit (LIHTC) allows corporations to invest in affordable housing production in return for an absolute credit on their income tax bills. Its success in Chicago has been tremendous, leveraging more than $151 million in private investment to

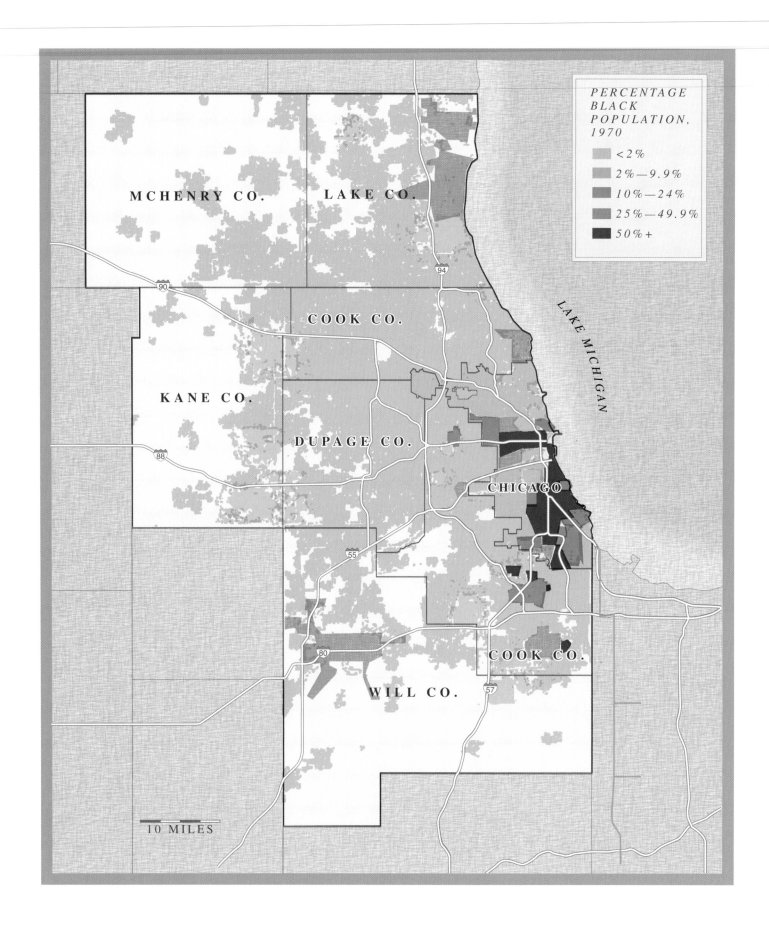

PERCENTAGE
BLACK
POPULATION,
1970

< 2%

2% — 9.9%

10% — 24%

25% — 49.9%

50% +

MCHENRY CO.

LAKE CO.

COOK CO.

KANE CO.

DUPAGE CO.

CHICAGO

COOK CO.

WILL CO.

LAKE MICHIGAN

10 MILES

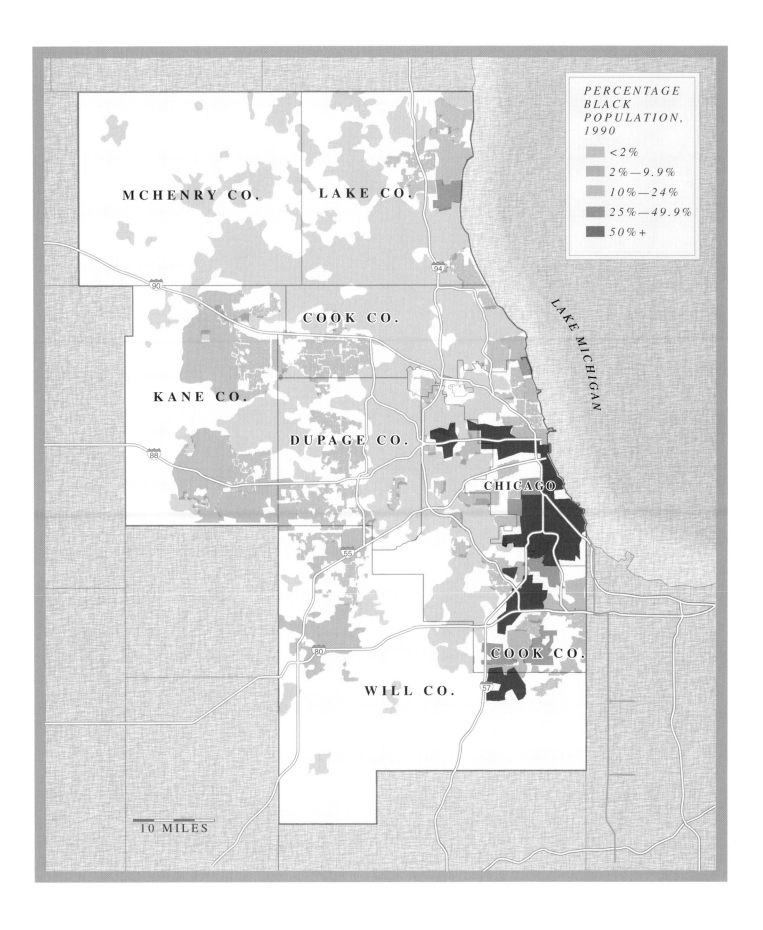

MCHENRY CO.

LAKE CO.

COOK CO.

KANE CO.

DUPAGE CO.

CHICAGO

LAKE MICHIGAN

COOK CO.

WILL CO.

*PERCENTAGE
BLACK
POPULATION,
1990*

< 2 %
2 % — 9.9 %
10 % — 24 %
25 % — 49.9 %
50 % +

10 MILES

produce 10,000 affordable homes and apartments for low-income families and individuals over an eight-year period (1987–1995). Nationally, the Housing Credit is responsible for 95 percent of all affordable housing being produced. Chicago annually awards $35 million in federal tax credits spread out over ten years. The total amount of tax credits is equal to $1.25 per resident per year. We recommend that the federal government affirm and expand the success of this tax credit by raising the per capita to $1.75 per resident per year.

COMMUNITY DEVELOPMENT CORPORATIONS

The work of community rebuilding over the last few decades suggests that without competent Community Development Corporations (CDCs) that are deeply rooted in low-income and segregated communities and that are capable of delivering results, inner-city communities cannot be transformed into livable and stable neighborhoods. Most of the 100 CDCs in this region specialize in economic development, subdivided into commercial and industrial development, and housing. In conjunction with intermediary organizations such as the Local Initiatives Support Corporation, and utilizing other funding mechanisms such as the LIHTC program, CDCs have been able to leverage enough funding to provide several million square feet of commercial/industrial space and roughly 10,000 units of affordable housing in Chicago's neighborhoods. These efforts have led to the rejuvenation of a number of communities throughout the city, including several that had long been written off in the public mind.

Metropolis 2020 recommends that corporations and foundations headquartered in this region facilitate the creation of strong networks (including shared computer learning centers) among CDCs in both the city and suburbs in order to build coalitions that can make sustainable economic and social prosperity a reality in the region.

BUILDING CREDITWORTHINESS

Individual Development Accounts (IDAs) are a new mechanism established by the federal government as a national pilot project to foster asset accumulation among welfare recipients, the working poor, and others who lack the resources to participate in traditional savings and investment programs.[2] The two Chicago institutions participating in this project are South Shore Bank (through a nonprofit affiliate) and Women's Self-Employment Project. Deposits by account holders to restricted savings accounts at these two institutions are matched by the participating institution two-to-one to jump-start their savings and enable them to purchase or leverage an asset within two years.[3] The initial matching funds and the funds for setting up the programs were provided by the federal government. This initial funding has since been supplemented by foundation grants. In addition, private employers are entitled to a

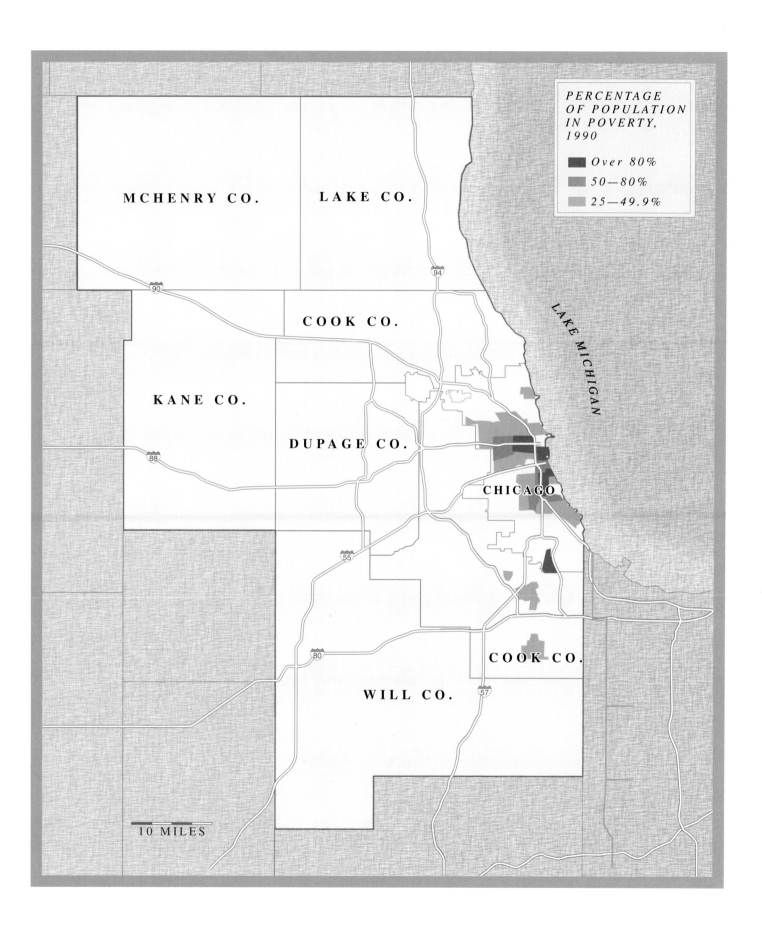

MCHENRY CO.

LAKE CO.

COOK CO.

LAKE MICHIGAN

KANE CO.

DUPAGE CO.

CHICAGO

COOK CO.

WILL CO.

10 MILES

federal income tax deduction with respect to matching contributions to their employees' accounts. We urge employers to take advantage of this feature of the project.

To attract prospective lower- and middle-income homebuyers with some acquired savings, many banks have adjusted their credit screens so that these households can qualify for mortgages they otherwise would have been denied because of a bad credit history or a high debt-to-income ratio. While many of these loans have been successful, their default ratio is higher than average. A 1996 survey[4] noted a correlation between the level of delinquencies and the number of years a bank had offered affordable mortgage loans. Among the common characteristics of banks with lower delinquency rates was a required comprehensive program of pre-purchase counseling as a prerequisite for qualifying for affordable mortgages.

In order to lower delinquency rates and the number of foreclosures to households with these affordable mortgages, it is recommended that the Community Renewal Act measurement criteria be revised to measure banks on the duration and quality of their loans in addition to the number of loans originated. In the near term, new families may not be prepared for homeownership, and, therefore, we support the delivery of accredited and standardized counseling that will help prospective buyers assess their finances and build their assets in order to invest responsibly in their communities.

FAIR HOUSING

Private-sector groups are urged to continue to press for vigorous enforcement of fair housing laws[5] and to establish a mechanism for testing throughout all parts of the housing market; education, outreach, and documentation about fair housing laws and remedies to housing discrimination; stronger monitoring and regulation of banking, real estate, appraisal, and insurance industry practices; and review and challenge of discriminatory municipal actions. The power of information to change practices should not be underestimated.

The business and foundation community should strongly support the continuing needs of the Leadership Council for Metropolitan Open Communities, which provides information and relocation counseling services to disadvantaged minorities; and those of Access Living of Metropolitan Chicago, which provides fair housing services to people with disabilities.

Providing Basic Mobility for the Poor

Freedom of movement is essential to equity of opportunity. Accordingly, once the RCC (the Regional Coordinating Council discussed in chapter 8) is up and running, it should be empowered to experiment with programs for meeting the basic mobility needs of the poor. Such programs could be facilitated by the use of electronic cards that are debited as used.

Low-income users' cards could be automatically credited each month, and the cards would give access both to public transit and to electronically priced roads and parking facilities. These subsidies could be funded with revenues derived from the various pricing measures imposed on private vehicle use.

At present, the Metra system is well geared to bringing suburbanites into downtown Chicago, but it is poorly designed to transport low-income residents in the city out to the suburbs where most of the entry-level jobs are created. Metra should be required, even in advance of the establishment of the RCC, to take all reasonable steps to remedy this situation. For example, new stations should be installed in the city at strategic points where low-income workers can board outgoing trains in the morning. Depending on the traffic generated, the frequency of train times can be increased to accommodate the demand for reverse commuting.

CHAPTER TEN

ENRICHING THE QUALITY OF LIFE

MOBILITY, LAND USE, AND THE ENVIRONMENT

*T*his plan is aimed at enhancing the basic social opportunities of all the region's residents to lead healthy, productive lives and enjoy a high quality of life. In this last chapter of part 2, we set forth a set of interrelated recommendations that, if implemented, will alter the spatial patterns and mobility structures of the region over the very long term so that all its residents, across the spectrums of race and income, can choose from a wide range of options as to where and in what kinds of homes to live and how to move about.

Personal Mobility

The key recommendations in this section are designed to ameliorate the problems that have arisen by reason of people's excessive reliance on private vehicle travel, as described in chapter 2; to motivate people to use other forms of mobility in place of or in tandem with the private vehicle; and to ensure that the region's land is used in ways that reduce mobility needs. At the same time, because the private vehicle will continue to be the chief means of surface transportation for the foreseeable future, the plan recognizes the need in the near term to invest in the road infrastructure and in intelligent transportation systems in consultation with experts in automotive technology.

PRICING THE MOTOR VEHICLE

"I've come to the conclusion what we really are faced with here is a systematic change from a pattern of uncontrolled sprawl toward a brand new path that makes quality of life the goal of all our urban, suburban and farmland policies."

⟷

AL GORE

There is no painless way to raise the additional $500 million per year we estimate will be necessary to meet the region's transportation needs, but the fairest way is by some combination of fuel taxes, pricing of road use, licensing and registration fees, and/or parking charges.[1] Half of this sum should be raised by the state to meet the capital and maintenance needs of the road system in the region, and the other half should be raised for transit purposes by the regional coordinating mechanism proposed in chapter 8.

There will, of course, be stiff opposition to higher taxes and fees on vehicles and vehicle use, but the goal of increased use of public transit cannot be attained until drivers are sent appropriate price signals as to the true costs of private vehicle travel. Moreover, these taxes and fees should be more than offset by the savings from privatizing transit and other transportation services as proposed below. At least half of the funds raised by these taxes and fees on the motor vehicle should be used to rehabilitate the region's transit system and undertake new projects in line with the priorities established by CATS.

Taxing motor vehicles to subsidize transit is justified because it ensures that the vast majority of residents—including people who are elderly, young, poor, or disabled—enjoy a basic level of urban mobility and also because mass transit reinforces the vibrancy of high-density centers both in the central business district of Chicago and also, increasingly, in retail/employment clusters in other parts of the region. The revenue-raising measures we propose will send the right signals to vehicle users and thereby encourage them to consider other mobility options and housing choices. As explained in the next subsection, these measures will also begin to raise the revenues required to adequately maintain the region's road system and enable the RTA over time to restore the region's transit system to a state of good condition.

IMPROVING PUBLIC TRANSIT

With the increased revenue sources, the region not only can pursue the transit projects identified in the 2020 RTP (CATS' regional transportation plan, described in chapter 2); it can assign higher priority to transit than does the 2020 RTP. By making transit a much more attractive option while also increasing the costs of driving, commuters will tend to change their habits, and the region's systems will gradually become more viable and begin to cover a larger proportion of their variable, if not fixed, costs. But for the foreseeable future, rail and other mass-transit systems will in most cases continue to require heavy subsidization.

One of the best ways to improve the attractiveness of transit is to provide connections between high-activity centers: adding pedways from Northwestern and Union stations to the CTA and the existing pedway system; developing a rectangle of dedicated bus lanes and new busways (streets or lanes for buses only) in the central business district of Chicago to link the train stations, the business offices and hotels in the Loop and North Michigan Avenue area, and the convention center; building more park 'n' ride parking lots and garages to connect to the RTA system; and developing intermodal stations where Metra and CTA trains are adjacent, such as at 35th and LaSalle Streets and at 35th Street and Archer Avenue.

In the same vein, the CATS proposal for adding two lanes to the thirteen-mile segment of I-90 (at a cost of $130 million) should be rejected. Instead, that right-of-way should be used for a new transit line that would extend the CTA Blue Line to Elk Grove, Schaumburg, Rolling Meadows, and beyond. These two lanes are the only available corridor for transit.[2]

This same stretch is a corridor of high job concentration, and priority should therefore be given to public transit. It would also allow for an intermodal connection (estimated to cost over $50 million) from the O'Hare people mover to the CTA and Metra. The most important benefits of this new link would be (1) to accommodate persons traveling from the north or northwest to O'Hare, (2) to provide better access to jobs located northwest of the airport, and (3) to provide easy access from the airport to the west Loop business district and to the convention center via new dedicated bus lanes from Union Station. This proposal should be reinforced with other, complementary strategies to encourage transit use.[3]

Van and car pools. Employers, unions, and community associations should work together to establish information facilities and provide incentives so that neighbors and fellow employees are motivated both to use public transit and to enter into ridesharing arrangements. Also, local governments should provide preferential parking for high-occupancy vehicles. In addition, we support the idea of experimenting with ramp bypass lanes to give priority to buses and high-occupancy vehicles over single-occupant vehicles as they proceed into the main traffic flow.

Paratransit. Given today's decentralized urban living patterns, a strong case can be made for transit services using vans, taxis, shuttle buses, and jitneys that do not follow fixed routes. They would provide non-capital-intensive alternatives to the monopoly of local transit authorities. A central switchboard and computer would match drivers and riders. A person requesting a ride would be matched in real time with a van company or, as a last resort, a taxi. Local regulations that prohibit or sharply restrict the establishment of private express commuter buses, jitneys, or van services would have to be abolished.

Aerial view of Riverside, a community designed by Frederick Law Olmstead in 1869.

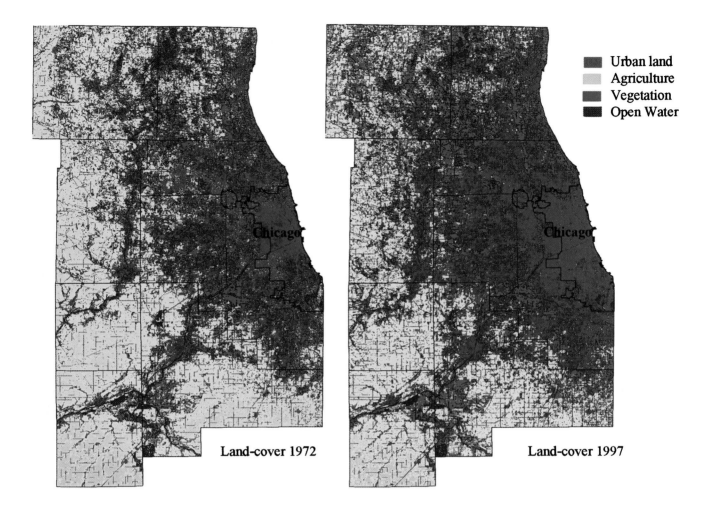

Urban land

Agriculture

Vegetation

Open Water

Land-cover 1972

Land-cover 1997

Urban land use change in metropolitan Chicago from 1972 to 1997, derived from Landsat Data.

Privatization. Public transit would also be improved if public agencies contracted with private firms to provide publicly sponsored and subsidized transit services in high-density areas. Cost savings of 20 to 30 percent have been realized in contracting out conventional fixed-route bus services. These savings would allow existing public subsidies to support a larger network of service. We urge the city to study the advantages of privatizing the entire CTA system. This seems to be the order of the day in Great Britain, New Zealand, and Australia, and it is working. We also believe that operating costs can be substantially reduced by privatization initiatives—for example, subcontracting out such services as bus, train, and station maintenance and cleaning.

Security. The CTA should experiment with electronics and other means to enhance the security of transit riders. Even if the price of automotive transportation increases, transit use will remain low as long as riders are apprehensive about their personal safety.

Moderating Mobility Needs

> "The most necessary, profound change in our visions is to recognize that only a variety of great concentrations strongly and permanently joined with expansive areas of dispersal will create for us the rich, accessible, diverse, communal, landscaped [region] we desire. . . . The future regional city must be a place where multiple centers of great density integrate work, commerce, culture, residence, and social services. That same city must also have regions of low-density development, expanses of single-family houses, parks, shopping, and other facilities and institutions that support the quality of life associated with the traditional green suburbs."
>
> MOSHE SAFDIE, ARCHITECT

EXPLOITING COMMUNICATIONS TECHNOLOGIES

We have only begun to recognize, much less exploit, the opportunities for moderating transportation needs through the application of computer and communications technologies. For example, while the productivity of people in the workplace will always require considerable face-to-face interaction, employers should look for creative ways in which to train employees to increase their effectiveness through telecommuting. As computer networking becomes more commonplace, this evolution can take place without public policy intervention. If only a small fraction of the nation's workforce were enabled to work from their homes for only one day each week, the social concerns stemming from motor vehicle use would be greatly alleviated. Moreover, communications technologies could significantly moderate mobility needs in other arenas such as education, shopping, entertainment, and the common pursuit of hobbies.

LAND-USE AND HOUSING STRATEGIES

One of the costs of low-density development is the amount of vehicle travel it entails: the long distances people must travel between home, work, shopping, and play. The strategies that we recommend for addressing these and other policy concerns associated with sprawl are aimed in part at achieving land-use and housing patterns over the long term that require much less travel. These strategies are set forth below.

For the near term, Intelligent Transportation Systems (ITSs) encompass a broad set of advanced technologies for collecting and using traffic and travel information to assist drivers in many ways. These systems have the ability to guide private vehicles around congested areas, improve their night vision, and warn drivers of impending collisions.

Advocates of ITS technology believe that it will someday be the basis of an automated highway system. Vehicles that operate as individual automobiles in the local street environment could become components of a high-speed, high-capacity, high-safety automated road system when engaged in longer trips on expressways. Because such an automated highway would have several times the capacity of the traditional roadway, much less urban space would be devoted compared to today's costly, disruptive urban freeway structures. It would have a safety level commensurate with the automated air transportation system, thereby removing a major deficiency of current vehicle technology, which must place a high priority on mass and crashworthiness. Thus, an urban vehicle mix could be established, dominated by smaller, lighter cars that consume much less energy and emit much less pollution.

Of course, there is ample reason to proceed with caution. For example, designing and testing a fail-safe automated highway could take decades. Also, increasing the carrying capacity of arterial roads could present new challenges for urban core areas that are unable to cope with present levels of parking and local traffic. Yet, ITSs have tremendous potential. Metropolis 2020, in consultation with the Metropolitan Mayors Caucus, should appoint a task force to work in consultation with experts in ITS technology, to the end of designing a state-of-the-art urban transportation system for the new century.

Protecting Open Space and Preserving Farmland

The Regional Greenways Plan, which is a joint project of NIPC and the Open Lands Project, is strongly endorsed. The plan's mission is to protect and connect a 4,300-mile system of stream-based and land-based greenways, with almost 2,000 miles of trails. The Greenways system builds on a major recommendation of the Burnham Plan, namely the protection of the several major water-related corridors through acquisition of hundreds of small, strategically located plots throughout the metropolitan area.

Since most of the Greenways system is dependent on the participation of major landowners and businesses located along the corridors, it is recommended that the state create appropriate incentives to encourage these individuals and businesses to make land easements available to help create these greenways. The benefits of expanding our regional greenways system will be less flooding, cleaner storm-water runoff, better water quality in our streams, broader biodiversity, less investment in public and private infrastructure, more recreational opportunities, better health and mental well-being, more attractive local and re- gional landscapes, higher property values, a sense of cooperation while preserving open space, and a legacy for those who will follow.

THE CHICAGO WILDERNESS PROGRAM

Metropolis 2020 strongly supports Chicago Wilderness, a program of the Chicago Region Biodiversity Council. Chicago Wilderness is a partnership of public and private organiza- tions that have joined forces to protect, restore, and manage the natural ecological commu- nities of the region. The Chicago region is the most populous metropolitan area in the Mid- west. At the same time, it is home to some of the rarest and most biologically diverse natural communities in the world. The region's landscape includes unique natural communities ranging from dunes complexes along the shores of Lake Michigan, to wooded communities along major waterways, to scattered remnant prairies and savannas. Its rivers and lakes sup- port one of the most diverse collections of wetlands on the continent. Protecting and restor- ing ecological health holds the promise of long-term sustainability in terms of both biol- ogy and a foundation for enhanced quality of life and economic health. The challenge is to protect key areas not yet in public ownership and enlarge and manage the protected areas to the extent that they can support the full range of ecological communities that comprise the natural habitat of northeastern Illinois. The region's protected natural habitats, with their waters, plants, and animals, share the name of the program that protects them: Chicago Wilderness.

LAND PRESERVATION AND TRANSFER OF DEVELOPMENT RIGHTS

Illinois should establish a land preservation program for the state, and it should have a sharp focus on northeastern Illinois. It might be similar to recent initiatives in other states such as the Green Acres Program in New Jersey or Maryland's Project Open Space and Rural Legacy Program. Both programs have dramatically increased funding for land ac- quisition in those states. Such an initiative should target critical natural areas that are under development pressure and facilitate the acquisition of lands to implement regional and local open-space plans in order to meet the growing outdoor recreation needs of this region. Budgets for forest-preserve and conservation districts should be funded to the fullest extent

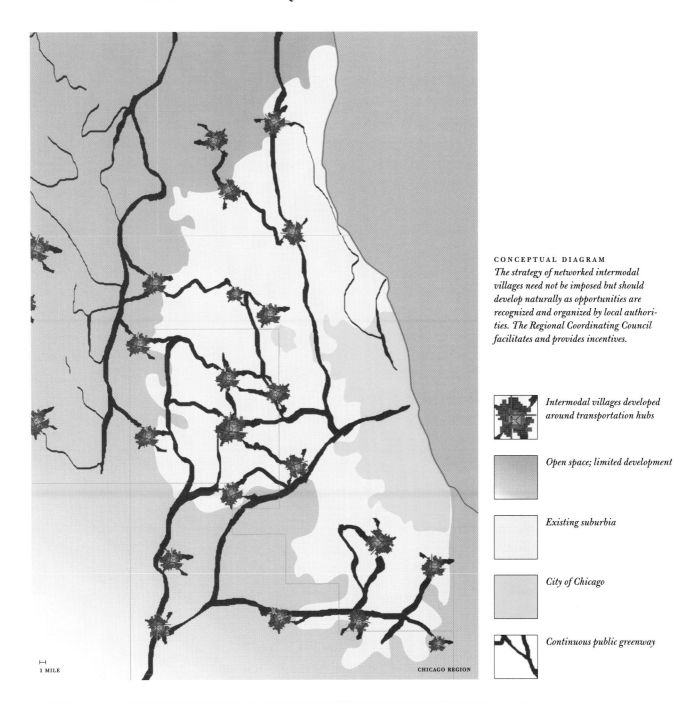

CHICAGO REGION

CONCEPTUAL DIAGRAM
The strategy of networked intermodal villages need not be imposed but should develop naturally as opportunities are recognized and organized by local authorities. The Regional Coordinating Council facilitates and provides incentives.

Intermodal villages developed around transportation hubs

Open space; limited development

Existing suburbia

City of Chicago

Continuous public greenway

possible under Illinois' current tax cap restrictions and, where necessary, referenda should be held to secure additional funding for land acquisition.

A variety of land-preservation strategies should be pursued, including acquisition of full ownership rights as well as purchase of conservation easements. In addition, state and local governments should reinforce private efforts to preserve open space, such as the donation of conservation easements and the establishment of conservation communities where open or resource-rich lands are permanently protected as critical components of a development plan. Corporations with large campuses should consider sustainable landscaping approaches that support biodiversity by incorporating native plant materials.

The preservation of open land on the urban fringe depends on choices made by both the private and public sectors. Farmers seeking to retire are sometimes beguiled by the prices developers are willing to pay for their land. Federal, state, and local policies also make development on the urban fringe an attractive opportunity. One way of addressing the loss of farmland and the demand for development on the outskirts of our region is the concept of transferable development rights. Under this concept, a developer can sometimes transfer "density" from adjacent properties if further development of them is restricted. The net result can be the same overall density but distributed differently between parcels of land. To formalize this process locally, we recommend that counties and local municipalities designate appropriate areas in their plans as eligible to sell and receive the transferable rights.

Increasing the Range of Housing Opportunities throughout the Region

A NEW STATE BUILDING CODE

Local building codes, with their many special requirements, often pose serious obstacles to the development of affordable housing throughout the region. In some cases, municipal building codes undermine the goals of energy conservation. Accordingly, we call for the adoption of a statewide building code that would supersede all local building codes.

EMPLOYER-ASSISTED HOUSING

Traditionally employers have invested in relocation assistance for top management, but an increasing number of employers are also instituting services for nonmanagerial and hourly employees. Employer-assisted housing programs can not only address labor shortages and the mismatch between housing and jobs, they can help working families attain decent, affordable housing; reduce turnover, hiring, and training costs; increase productivity; minimize employee lateness/absenteeism; boost employee morale and loyalty; and improve the employer's public image.

There are a variety of models for assisting employees in identifying housing resources. Some employers actively advocate particular housing developments that would help their employees, while nonprofit groups provide counseling and better access to affordable mortgages to area employees.

Metropolis 2020 intends, early on, to establish a task force to develop and test the viability of a proposal for a new social compact that would be entered into by major employers in the region. The compact would obligate the signatories to give strong weight, in arriving at decisions respecting the location, relocation, and expansion of new offices and facilities in northeastern Illinois, to the following factors: (1) Whether the locality has provided for the creation of adequate amounts of housing that are affordable by middle-income households (those with incomes between 80 percent and 120 percent of the median household income in the region); and (2) Whether the locality is exerting reasonable efforts (a) to curtail unlimited low-density development, and, (b) where feasible, to permit and encourage compact development for commercial, residential, and other purposes near public rail-transit stations.

The task force should develop a definitive proposal and conduct a survey among major employers in the region as to their readiness to enter into such a compact and as to any changes they would suggest to make the compact more effective. If the results of this survey are sufficiently favorable, Metropolis 2020 should then take the initiative in seeing that this compact is signed onto by as many area employers as possible.

T H E   R O L E   O F   T H E   R C C

The RCC (the Regional Coordinating Council, discussed in chapter 8), once established, should use the recommended incentive program to encourage the provision of housing throughout the region for all economic segments of the population. Most of the housing in both Chicago and the suburbs would tend to be concentrated in mixed-use developments in or near intermodal transportation hubs.

Putting the Pieces Together

Consider how the Netherlands' Randstad Holland has developed over the last half century. Randstad Holland, which means "the ring city," is that complex urban agglomeration located in the provinces of North and South Holland. The Randstad is made up of fifteen or twenty cities, almost all of which have ancient origins. It is comparable in population and territorial size to metropolitan Chicago, but the distribution of residential life and economic activity is quite different. Unlike the Chicago region, the growth and dispersion of economic activity in the Randstad has not taken place in a growing amorphous ring around one city. Rather it has been distributed among four major cities—Amsterdam, Rotterdam,

The Hague, and Utrecht—and another dozen or so smaller cities; together these cities take the shape of a large horseshoe. The heart of the horseshoe is protected agricultural space (known as the "Green Heart"). In short, it is one of the world's few multicentered metropolises and one of the few metropolises of any kind that has done such a superb job of protecting important agricultural lands and open space.

In part, this phenomenon is a matter of historical accident. Yet the economic and demographic forces that have been such important factors in reshaping the American metropolis along low-density lines since World War II have been at least as powerful in the case of Randstad Holland. It was only by virtue of strong land-use policies put in place beginning in 1945 that the Netherlands was able to maintain the Randstad as a multicentered metropolis and to protect its open space. One of those policies called for the creation of buffer zones to separate the different cities. A second policy was aimed at preserving the agricultural heart of the Randstad "horseshoe." A third policy called for more compact use of existing built-up areas.

These techniques are not foreign to America. Oregon, Washington, and (more recently) Maryland have instituted interesting and quite different approaches to the challenge of managing growth. So have a small fraction of cities and counties across the nation. Their approaches are in stark contrast to the vision of unlimited low-density development that has been so dominant in our country for the last several decades—the vision pursued in the extreme by a number of major cities in the western and southwestern United States.

The "Green Heart"—the center of Randstad Holland, a multicentered metropolis.

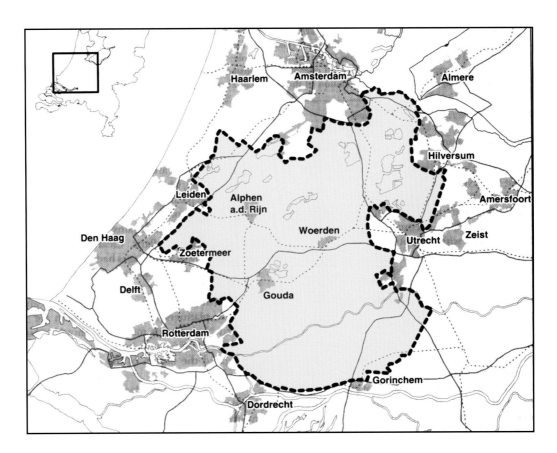

While Randstad Holland is not Utopia, it provides something of a model in terms of how it has used its land to protect the natural environment and enhance the quality of life of its residents.

Suppose that the vast majority of the Chicago region's population decided that more people should have more choices, both as to where and in what kinds of housing to live and also as to the various modes by which to make their daily trips. They might be compelled to want such freedom of choice out of a desire to budget their time more wisely, to spend less time in lengthy commutes, to enjoy the cosmopolitan life in a suburban setting, to spend more time with family, to live lives that are more hassle-free, and to spend less time caring for their private property and more time enjoying public spaces.

Such a major cultural shift is not unthinkable. Consider, for example, the sudden shift in thinking about environmental issues following the publication in 1962 of Rachel Carson's *Silent Spring.* As another example, few in the late 1950s foresaw the hugely successful civil rights movement that took place only a few years later.

There are many possible scenarios that one could envision fifty years hence if such a cultural shift were to take place and if the tools recommended in this plan were in place. One thing we can be sure about, though, is that the region's mobility structures will continue to have a profound effect on spatial patterns. Thus, if the RCC were even partially successful in creating intermodal transportation hubs in the region and bringing about large mixed-use developments surrounding these hubs, more suburban residents would choose to live and work in one of these intermodal villages.

To illustrate, an intermodal village of 150,000 to 200,000 people living in an area of 16 to 18 square miles would have the critical mass to support a variety of mobility options. The low-density areas in the outer ring might accommodate 4 to 6 households per acre on average, for a total of 65,000 to 85,000 people. The medium-high-density areas could accommodate 10 to 12 units per acre, for a total of 30,000 to 45,000 people. Finally, the highest-density housing in the village center, consisting of medium rises (of up to 8 stories) and duplexes, might accommodate 55,000 to 70,000 people.

The present forms of zoning by type of use might eventually be superseded by laws that focus on proximity to public transit and intermodal centers, and prevention of noise, undesirable odors, and pollution. Owners of detached single-family homes near transit/shopping centers might be given special zoning permission and tax incentives to build garage apartments for smaller, second households.

The vast majority of suburbs would continue to develop along present lines, but at least people would have clear choices in a free market. Some would choose to live in one of the intermodal villages, attracted by their ability to utilize each mode of mobility to its maximum advantage, with convenient means of transferring from one mode to another. For example, those living in or near the village center would rely heavily on walking and bicycling, particularly where there is no need for transporting heavy parcels. Those living in any area of an intermodal village would utilize subcompact personal community vehicles (PCVs) for short trips (say ten minutes or less) into the village center or other parts of the village when

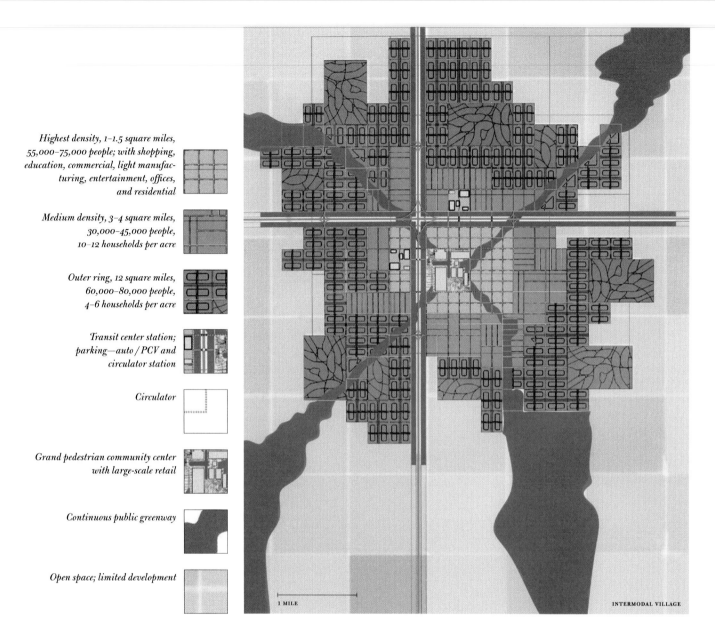

Highest density, 1–1.5 square miles, 55,000–75,000 people; with shopping, education, commercial, light manufacturing, entertainment, offices, and residential

Medium density, 3–4 square miles, 30,000–45,000 people, 10–12 households per acre

Outer ring, 12 square miles, 60,000–80,000 people, 4–6 households per acre

Transit center station; parking—auto / PCV and circulator station

Circulator

Grand pedestrian community center with large-scale retail

Continuous public greenway

Open space; limited development

1 MILE

INTERMODAL VILLAGE

the weather is inclement or when there is a need to transport bulky items. The PCV might be powered by batteries or some hybrid system, or eventually by fuel cells. It would be an ultra-low or zero polluter, and it would seat up to four people. The back seat could be folded down for extra storage capacity. All PCVs, by virtue of being subcompact, could be parked without charge on the periphery of the village center and at low rates within the center. All other vehicles could be parked at higher rates on the periphery and at very high rates in the center.

Both downtown Chicago and the intermodal village centers would have circulator systems (either fixed rail or bus). People would switch conveniently from their parked vehicles on the periphery and take the circulator to within a five-minute walk of their destination. These centers would feature a complex of outlets for retail goods and personal services where people could do their errands in the process of shifting from one mode of travel to another.

Three views of urban sprawl: 1915 (top); the present (middle); and a projection for 2020 (bottom). Note the intermodal villages clustered at the outskirts of the city in the projection for 2020.

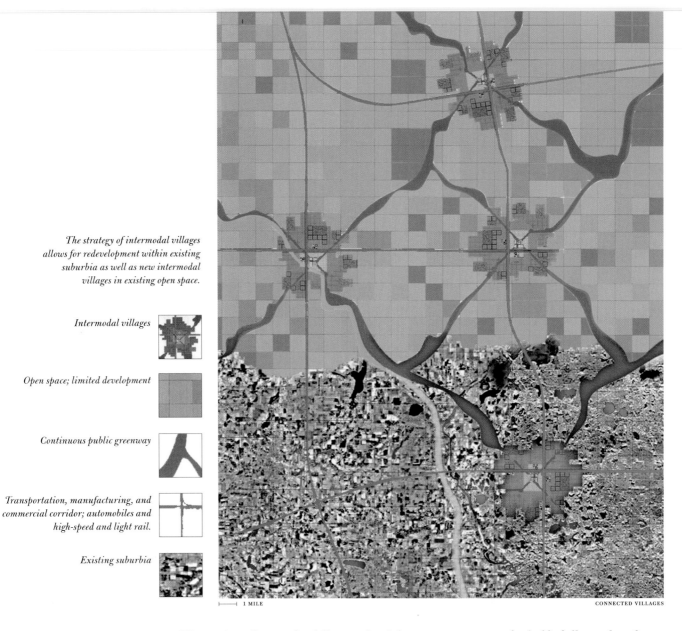

The strategy of intermodal villages allows for redevelopment within existing suburbia as well as new intermodal villages in existing open space.

Intermodal villages

Open space; limited development

Continuous public greenway

Transportation, manufacturing, and commercial corridor; automobiles and high-speed and light rail.

Existing suburbia

1 MILE

CONNECTED VILLAGES

The various forms of public transit might come to account for half of all travel to, from, and within the cores of Chicago and the intermodal villages. This much higher level of transit use would emerge as various mechanisms for the pricing of private vehicle use were introduced in these core areas and as ingenious initiatives were introduced to make public transit much speedier than the car in high-density areas: for example, traffic lights that automatically turn green for approaching buses and trams in preference to private vehicles at intersections, and dedicated lanes reserved for trams, buses, taxis, and emergency vehicles.

For years to come, many—probably most—people will prefer to live in a detached single-family home in a traditional suburb or city neighborhood and continue to rely on the motor vehicle as their chief, almost exclusive, form of mobility. But we should plan for the likelihood, over the longer term, that more and more people will prefer to have a range of choices as to where and in what kinds of homes to live and how to move about.

OUTREACH AND

IMPLEMENTATION

CHICAGO METROPOLIS 2020 AND THE FUTURE OF THE PLAN

*I*n the course of the study project leading up to the issuance of this plan, the members of the Commercial Club have reached out to many in the public, private, and nonprofit sectors, including religious leaders and leaders in government and higher education, and to the many outstanding civic organizations throughout the six-county region. We have profited greatly from their insights and suggestions.

We each have differing and complementary roles to play in working toward the goals of the plan. Faith communities have been involved in almost every major struggle for justice in our region and in the nation, and have historically been able to facilitate racial integration when others have failed. The most important breakthroughs in this area have been brought about by grassroots efforts. We urge these communities to educate and sensitize all residents of the region to their moral and social obligations to take the initiative in bringing about an era of greater mutual understanding among people of different ethnic and racial backgrounds.

Educators can enable their students to see the implications of these ideals for the life of the community and the health of the economy. Business, labor, civic, and government leaders can create the sort of public/private partnerships that served us so well in the early decades of this century. Such partnerships are more essential today than ever in light of the devolution of federal powers and responsibilities now under way.

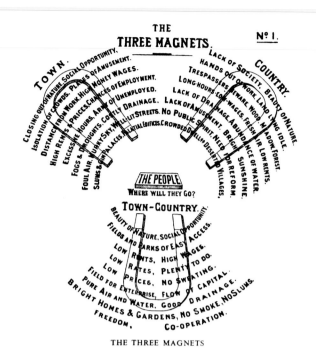

THE THREE MAGNETS

To these ends, given the fluid, dynamic nature of the circumstances in which concrete-action plans must be developed, and given the fact that this plan is intended to serve as a springboard for generating public discussion and policy reform in the state and in the region over the next twenty years or more, the Commercial Club created, in early 1999, a new civic organization. This new organization shares the name of the plan—Chicago Metropolis 2020 (or simply Metropolis 2020)—and it is unlike any of the many other charitable and community groups in the Chicago region.

Led by a large and diverse Executive Council composed of leaders from all parts of the region, Metropolis 2020 is already becoming a catalyst for the debate and implementation of many of the recommendations in the plan.

Metropolis 2020 brings many different voices, opinions, and areas of expertise to the table. About half the members of its Executive Council are also members of the Commercial Club. In addition to this organizational support, the Commercial Club is providing generous funding to Metropolis 2020. The strong participation by Commercial Club members signals the depth of their commitment to the plan's implementation.

Having filled the remainder of the seats on the Executive Council with leaders from organized labor, civic organizations, universities, faith communities, and state and local governments, the members of the Commercial Club appreciate that the work ahead must bring as many leaders as possible into in the discussion and implementation phases of this project.

Metropolis 2020 is headed by two prominent Commercial Club members, Andrew J. McKenna and George A. Ranney, Jr.

During its inaugural year of operation, Metropolis 2020 determined that its first priority is to foster collaboration across the six-county region and take actions that will strengthen the economic vitality of life in the region. They set out to make our region one of the places in the world where people most want to live and work.

In the early weeks of its founding, Metropolis 2020 helped organize a coalition of other civic organizations and government leaders to work on behalf of a historic state legislative package addressing road, transit, and other infrastructure improvements needed throughout Illinois. The $12 billion Illinois FIRST program, which was advocated by Governor George H. Ryan and approved by the General Assembly in the spring of 1999, went a long way toward resolving the backlog of needed highway improvements and transit infrastructure problems in the region.

The legislative victory demonstrated the ability and potential of this new regional catalyst to shine a spotlight on critical problems and organize a diverse, collaborative team of civic entrepreneurs to champion new solutions to those challenges.

Metropolis 2020 has created several working groups to examine some of the issues in the plan and to build support for solutions. Those efforts include groups that focus on expanding the link between transportation and land use; improving and expanding child-care opportunities for work-

"There is no stronger appeal made to the American citizen of today than comes from the call of one's native or adopted city to enter upon the service of creating better surroundings not only for one's self, but for all those who must of necessity earn their bread in the sweat of their brows. Nor is the call of posterity to be denied. To love and render service to one's city, to have a part in its advancement, to seek to better its conditions and to promote its higher interests, these are both the duty and the privilege of the patriot of peace."

DANIEL H. BURNHAM

ing families; developing a preventive health project; addressing the competition among municipalities for commercial tax base; and examining ways to bring coordination to the fragmented workforce training system.

It also began developing a set of "Metropolis Principles" along the lines of the social compact called for in the plan (see chapter 10). Metropolis 2020 will call on businesses and communities to embrace these principles, which will emphasize the need for a wide range of housing choices and easy access to mass transit for employees of new and expanding businesses.

Metropolis 2020 recognizes the need to educate citizens about the challenges outlined in this report and to engage as many people as possible in improving the region. It has hosted a series of community forums designed to increase the region's understanding of the challenges and work of Metropolis 2020 and to create several shared goals for the region.

Each goal will be translated into progress indicators that can be measured on an annual basis. This new "Regional Report Card" will allow the region to see where it is making progress toward the goals of the plan, and where it is not, and it will help the leadership of Metropolis 2020 determine its priorities into the future.

In a salute to the legacy and success of Daniel Burnham, Chicago Metropolis 2020 decided to create the twenty-first-century equivalent of *Wacker's Manual of the Plan of Chicago* (a "teacher's handbook," first printed in 1911).[1] Using the most advanced technology available, this new interactive educational tool will reach both adult citizens and young students in our schools, and help them learn what we need to do to make the Chicago region one of the world's most desirable places to live and work.

THE STORY OF THE PLAN OF 1909

It was in the late 1890s that Daniel Burnham began to test and refine his ideas for an ambitious plan for Chicago. In the spring of 1897, he presented papers to the Commercial Club and the younger Merchants' Club. Both clubs were composed of members of the Chicago business community. And they shared the same goals of improving Chicago's economic, civic, and cultural life.

Burnham argued the intrinsic value of art and beauty for all people in all kinds of environments, and he reminded his audiences that aesthetic and environmental reform could have stupendous benefits for Chicago's commercial and financial growth as well. There were no contradictions, he maintained, between beauty, efficiency, and material prosperity in other great cities of the world.

What kinds of prosperity should Chicago foster and maintain, Burnham asked rhetorically. "Not that for rich people solely or principally," he argued, "for they can take care of themselves and wander where they will in the pursuit of happiness; but the prosperity of those who must have employment in order to live. Do not these latter depend upon the circulation among them of plenty of ready money, and can this be brought about without the presence of large numbers of well-to-do people?" In proposing reforms, it seemed to Burnham, "evident at the outset that to attain a satisfactory result, we should aim at nothing less than a supreme improvement, that no half-way measure will do; that if we must lead, we must not be niggardly in what we undertake for Chicago."

The story told in this appendix is excerpted, almost word for word, from chapter 14 of Thomas Hines's 1974 award-winning biography, *Burnham of Chicago,* copyright © 1974 by Oxford University Press, Inc. Used by permission of Oxford University Press, Inc.

The clubs received the speech with interest, but Burnham realized that many more such efforts on his part would be necessary before a general enthusiasm would emerge to stimulate concerted action. Whenever possible, he urged the leaders of Chicago to work with him toward promoting a plan for the city's physical renewal. Little else happened, however; the club meetings of 1897 were the last large show of interest in the project for several years.

After nine years of frustration and delay, first the Merchants' Club and later the Commercial Club began to show real interest. Rather than compete with each other over the role of sponsor of the project, they decided in late 1906 to merge and work together on the Burnham proposal.

Burnham spent practically all of 1907 and 1908 in Chicago working on the plan. His assistant was Edward Bennett, who directed a staff of draftsmen and artists. Between April 1907, when the committees were appointed, and the end of February 1908, ninety-two regular and largely attended Committee meetings were held. In addition there were at least two hundred conferences with various public officials, including the Governor, the Mayor, the Park Boards and many others.

To carry on their deliberations, planners and committeemen needed information about Chicago, and Burnham and his staff took responsibility for obtaining it. Hundreds of requests for information and professional advice left Burnham's office in 1907 and 1908. He was equally interested in the smaller details of Chicago's economic, social, and cultural life, especially in such matters as transportation, health, and educational needs.

By late 1908, the plan was ready for the printer, and, by early summer of the following year, it was finally ready for distribution. It appeared with deliberate symbolic intent on July 4, 1909. "The Chicago Plan is out, and has caused a sensation," Burnham wrote to a friend on July 8. "The drawings are beautifully displayed in the Art Institute." Later in the month, he wrote that the plan seemed "successful even beyond our hopes."

Sumptuously printed by the Lakeside Press, *The Plan of Chicago* was a beautiful and elegant book. The drawings and watercolors by Jules Guerin and the black and white sketches by Jules Janin nicely complemented Bennett's maps and Burnham's text, as edited by [Charles] Moore. Fortunately, however, its scope and significance even transcended its aesthetic success. "Chicago in common with other great cities," Burnham's introduction began, "realizes that the time has come to bring order out of chaos incident to rapid growth, and especially to the influx of people of many nationalities without common traditions or habits of life. . . . The real test of the plan will be found in its application. If the plan is really good it will commend itself to the progressive spirit of the times, and . . . will be carried out. It should be understood, however, that such radical changes as are proposed herein cannot possibly be realized immediately. Indeed the aim has been to anticipate the needs of the future as well as to provide for the necessities of the present."

He reminded his readers that "during the second half of the nineteenth century the population of Chicago increased from thirty thousand to two millions of people. Today all conditions point to continued gains. The days of chance and uncertainty are past. The days of doubtful ventures are gone and the hazards of new fortunes. The elements which make for the greatness of the city are known to be permanent; and men realize that the time has now come to build confidently on foundations already laid." The lines that followed those observations were perhaps the most thoughtful and sensitive in the whole report. "The growth of the city," he wrote, "has been so rapid that it has been impossible to plan for the economical disposition of the great influx of people, surging like a human tide to spread itself wherever opportunity for profitable labor offered place. Thoughtful people are appalled at the results of progress; at the waste in time, strength, and money which congestion in city streets begets; at the toll of lives taken by disease when sanitary precautions are neglected; and at the frequent outbreaks against law and order which result from narrow and pleasureless lives. So that while the keynote of the nineteenth century was expansion, we of the twentieth century find that our dominant idea is conservation.

"The people of Chicago have ceased to be impressed by rapid growth or the great size of the city. What they insist asking now is: How are we living? Are we in reality prosperous? Is the city a convenient place for business? Is it a good labor market in the sense that labor is sufficiently comfortable to be efficient and content? Will the coming generation be able to stand the nervous strain of city life? When a competence has been accumulated, must we go elsewhere to enjoy the fruits of independence? If the city does not become better as it becomes bigger, shall not the defect be remedied?"

The plan called for the redevelopment of the whole Chicago area within a sixty-mile radius of the city's center, including an elaborate system of outer parks and radial and concentric boulevards; an aesthetic and useful lakefront park system twenty miles long along Lake Michigan; an increase in the number of and quality of interior parks; a grouping and relocation of railroad tracks and terminals; the straightening of the Chicago River for more efficient water and riverside transportation; myriad changes in the width, construction, function, and general appearance of individual streets, both grid and radial; a monumental civic center at the intersection of Halsted and Congress streets designed to mark the city's future center of gravity; and an efficient inner harbor development, enclosed by windbreaking causeways stretching a mile out into the lake. The plan called for an enlarged, cleared, and improved central passageway between north and south sides through the Loop while bringing the West Side into a closer and more convenient relationship with the rest. It envisioned a system then unsurpassed in America of connecting the city's center with its outlying suburbs and of linking the suburbs one with another.

Criticized in later years for his typical Progressive over-reliance on the efficacy of parks and for his failure in the plan to come to terms with the problems of slum and ghetto housing, Burnham acknowledged in the plan's early stages that parks were only a partial solution for the problem of the slums. Leaving indeed the vexing housing problem to other hands and later generations, he alluded to it significantly in what was perhaps the most radical statement in the report: "Chicago has not yet reached the point where it will be necessary for the municipality to provide at its own expense, as does the city of London, for the rehousing of people forced out of congested quarters, but unless the matter shall be taken in hand at once, such a course will be required in common justice to men and women so degraded by long life in the slums that they have lost all power of caring for themselves."

The local and national response to the plan was overwhelmingly favorable. One friend especially admired "the breadth of the ideas and the magnificence of the conception. . . . It is given to some of us to plod along with the more material every day wants of life, and we can only pause to appreciate the fact there are men in the community who have time, thought, interest, and genius enough to look forward to the larger needs of the community. It will always be of intense interest to me to follow in every way possible the working out of this great project, and I trust that in some small way I may be able to help it along."

Having taken the lead in initiating and producing the Chicago Plan, Burnham felt that others should take responsibility for its long and complex implementation. The ultimate success and efficacy of the plan demanded, he felt, that he not be the one to advocate his own proposals. In November 1909, after officially receiving the plan as a gift to the city from the Commercial Club, Mayor Fred Busse appointed a 328-member planning commission to give advice on and oversee future Chicago development along the guidelines of Burnham's proposals. Much in the same manner in which Burnham had earlier inspired Chicago's leaders to accept the plan, the commission began to inspire and to solicit the support of the people of Chicago. Through numerous pamphlets, a two-reel motion picture, a slide lecture series, and various other promotion devices, the Chicago Plan idea entered the home and the marketplace. The Chicago School Board agreed to use an elementary version of Burnham's report as an eighth-grade civics textbook. Ministers and rabbis throughout the city agreed to preach sermons in their churches and synagogues incorporating the ideas championed in the plan.

The most important years of the plan's realization occurred in the two decades between its publication in 1909 and the beginning of the Great Depression in 1929. Although elements of the scheme would continue to unfold throughout the century, the most significant projects took form in the 1920s. In the teens and twenties alone, costs of execution exceeded $300,000,000. Typical of the developments in that important period were such crucial projects as the early and precedent-setting widening of Twelfth Street, later renamed Roosevelt Road; the broadening and enrichment of upper Michigan Avenue above Randolph Street and north of the river; the building of Wacker Drive and the various riverfront facilities and accoutrements; and, perhaps most important, the landfill development of Grant Park and the long stretch of Lake Michigan shoreline to the north and south. Created on new land east of the old Illinois Central tracks, the vast lakeshore area from Grant to Jackson Park served both recreation and circulation functions and was named Burnham Park in honor of its patron.

Though facing inevitable alterations over the long span of its enactment, Burnham's Chicago Plan formed the basic outlines of the city's development and expansion in the twentieth century. For various and generally defensible reasons, the grandiose civic center proposed for the nexus of Halsted and Congress Streets never came to fruition, although a central traffic interchange and an even greater building complex would later occupy that area in the form of a Chicago campus for the University of Illinois. The successfully realized parts of the plan centered, for the most part, on Burnham's recommendations for the shoreline, the parks, the river, and street and circulation systems. Broad enough to allow room for growth and flexibility, yet detailed enough to provide specific direction, the plan became something of a model effort, influencing the plans for numerous other cities, both in America and abroad.

Commercial Club members often brought their visiting business associates to see the works. One such visitor asked: "How does it happen that you men of Chicago can get together and do such things? We cannot in New York, nor can the men of any other city."

In speaking years later to a London audience, Frank Lloyd Wright shocked his listeners by insisting that Chicago was the world's most beautiful city. When asked to justify his claim, he argued, "first of all because it has a generous park system, the greatest on earth. You may drive nearly all day without going away from the boulevard and park system. . . . Another reason is that, thanks to . . . Dan Burnham, Chicago seems to be the only great city in our States to have discovered its own waterfront. Moreover, to a greater extent than any other city, it has a life of its own."

U N D E R S T A N D I N G
S P R A W L   A N D
S E G R E G A T I O N

Sprawl

Urban sprawl, or unlimited low-density development, took place in three waves: first came the massive suburbanization of homes across America beginning after World War II; then followed the "malling" of the suburbs, beginning in the 1960s; and finally, beginning in the 1970s, came the relocation of jobs to the suburbs, where most urbanites have now lived and shopped for twenty-five years. Today, two-thirds of all American office facilities are in suburban centers, and 80 percent of those facilities have materialized only in the last two decades.

In 1950, according to Witold Rybczynski, "seven out of ten Americans living in metropolitan areas lived inside the limits of the main central city. Forty years later the situation has reversed, and now only four out of ten live in central cities." By 1990, "only half as many Americans nationwide were making the traditional suburb-to-city trip as were traveling from home to workplace without leaving the suburbs. The relationship between suburb and city has changed radically, from one of simple dependency to uneasy parity" (*City Life*, 1995).

In 1970, Chicago accounted for 48 percent of the region's population and nearly 60 percent of its jobs. Twenty years later, the city had 38 percent of the people and 37 percent of the jobs. In the metropolitan area, while the region's population grew by only 4 percent from 1970 to 1990, residential land consumption increased by 46 percent, and commercial and industrial land consumption increased by 74 percent. Whereas Northwest Suburban Cook County and DuPage County each had about 10 percent as many jobs as Chicago in 1970, today they each have about 40 percent as many.

TECHNOLOGY FACTORS

It was the motor vehicle that made obsolete the old radial patterns of metropolitan settlement along the lines of streetcar and railroad systems. The nation's vehicle population went from about fifty million in 1950, or about one vehicle for every three persons, to two hundred million in 1995, or about four vehicles for every five persons.

The decentralizing effects of the motor vehicle were compounded by other crucial technologies: the electrical system that gave every point in the region equal access to power; the telephone that provided instant communication from any point to any other point; and television, which is inherently decentralized and home centered.

> *"The end of World War I found Chicago poised for a new decade of extraordinary growth. . . . A new skyline rose above the Loop; outlying areas in the city filled up quickly; the rapidly increasing use of the automobile produced a whole new set of suburbs; and over 60,000 persons were added to the municipal population each year."*
>
> HAROLD M. MAYER AND RICHARD C. WADE, *CHICAGO,* 1969

ECONOMIC AND DEMOGRAPHIC FACTORS

Since 1950, the number of households has grown from 43.5 million to 97 million, thanks in part to the 65 percent increase in the population, in part to the increase in single-parent households (due to rising rates of divorce and births out of wedlock) and in part to the six-fold increase in single-person households among people aged twenty-five to forty-four. Most important, during this period, per capita disposable income (in constant dollars) increased by two and a half times, and the female civilian labor force more than tripled in size, roughly from 17 million to 56 million. In short, more people sought and could afford bigger homes on larger lots further away from work, school, and shopping, along with the greater vehicle travel this lifestyle entailed.

The resources for undertaking the massive dispersal of households and business facilities were readily at hand: an ample supply of labor and vast quantities of inexpensive land. Moreover, this period saw the rise of the entrepreneurs who built Levittown, Framingham, Southfield, and Oakbrook. They, like the rest of corporate America, were simply bringing to market new products that American consumers wanted at prices they could afford.

Beyond government-guaranteed loans to homebuyers, financing was made available on a larger scale than ever before to land speculators, builders, and fully integrated development companies. The capital came from insurance companies, depository institutions, and (indirectly) from a booming tax-exempt municipal bond market. Until 1986, private investors participated through tax shelters. In the late 1980s, the capital came increasingly from pension funds and off-shore investors. In the 1990s, the investing public began to fund real estate development again via the Real Estate Investment Trust. Everything, from factory outlet stores to "power-centers" anchored by Kmart and Wal-Mart, is now funded by publicly traded companies.

PUBLIC-POLICY FACTORS

The dispersal of the metropolis was facilitated by a host of policies at all levels of government. It was the Federal Housing Administration (FHA), created in 1934, that put the suburban home within reach of millions of citizens. It did so by insuring private mortgage lenders against loss on home loans stretching out to thirty years and with down payments of less than 10 percent. Lower risk meant that lenders could lend to more people and charge less interest. Also, interest was tax-deductible. All in all, it became cheaper to buy than to rent. Home ownership rose from 43.6 percent of all households in 1940 to 61.9 percent in 1960, after which it grew much more slowly. The great bulk of these guaranteed loans went for single-family homes in the suburbs.

The interstate highway system, begun in the 1950s, created both radial and circumferential arteries within metropolitan areas, making every part of the region readily accessible. Furthermore, vehicle travel was heavily subsidized, and it still is. Suburban residents going to work in major central business districts in the United States in their own vehicles directly pay for only about 25 percent of the total costs of their transport. The other 75 percent is typically borne by their employers (for example, in providing free parking), by other users (in increased congestion, reduced safety, etc.), by fellow workers or residents (in air or noise pollution, etc.), and by governments (passed on to the taxpayers of one generation or another in ways that bear no relationship to their amount of automotive travel). Revenues based on vehicle use cover only 60 percent of the costs of building and maintaining roads and bridges. Other items are also funded without regard to vehicle use: traffic-related police services, courts, and emergency vehicles. Moreover, employer-provided parking is subsidized through federal tax policy.

When a good as central to American life as the automobile remains underpriced for several decades, that good tends to be used more than it otherwise would be. Habits become ingrained and are hard to break. They are reinforced by the present urban infrastructure designed to exploit the full possibilities of private car mobility. The legacy is a built environment and a deeply rooted culture that for the next ten to twenty years leave metropolitan residents with little choice but to continue to rely chiefly on the motor vehicle for both private and public transportation.

Public policy also influenced the relocation of business operations. By the 1970s, businesses began to feel the brunt of the increasing taxes and over-regulation imposed in the central city. For Chicago, this situation was, and still is, exacerbated by the burden of Cook County's property tax classification on commercial and industrial properties. Many found that by moving to a hospitable suburb they could cut their local taxes in half. Other factors combined to create an environment hostile to business in older central cities. The federal government had long encouraged businesses to abandon older but very useable structures by permitting greater tax benefits for new construction than for the improvement of existing buildings. Even where tax credits were available for rehabilitating old historic industrial and commercial buildings in the central city, the developers in such cases almost always converted such buildings to residential use in order to maximize the return on their investment.

HUMAN ASPIRATIONS AND CULTURAL FACTORS

The car and other distance-reducing technologies, demographic and economic factors, and flawed public policies all help explain the phenomenon of sprawl, but they did not cause it. They merely enabled people to better approximate their dreams. City-dwelling households dreamed of release from urban crime and congestion, small quarters, and noise. They dreamed of a single-family home with a spacious yard and an attached garage to accommodate their two cars. And they dreamed of a safe and nurturing neighborhood in which to raise their children and live near their kind of people.

The suburban dream has deep roots. America's individualism, noted Tocqueville in *Democracy in America,* is "a calm and considered feeling which disposes each citizen to isolate himself from the mass of his fellows and withdraw into the circle of family and friends; with this little society formed to his taste, he gladly leaves the greater society to look after itself." Tocqueville, according to Rybczynski, "was pointing out another unique characteristic of the New World city: it was a setting for individual pursuits rather than communal activities" (*City Life*).

THE MOTIVATIONS OF BUSINESS

Retailers moved to the suburbs in pursuit of their customers. Why the lag for nonretail businesses? First, the advent of the interstate highway system meant that it was relatively easy for suburban workers to commute to the central city. The market and technology forces described above did not converge in great strength until the late 1970s. Second, business leaders tend to be highly visible by virtue of their positions of civic leadership in the central city. They are hesitant to appear to be abdicating their responsibilities. Finally, it is costly to relocate major operations. Such moves tended to be deferred until the case against staying put became overwhelming.

When the time did come, managers were driven, as always, by considerations of efficiency, productivity, and organizational morale. Industrial and distribution facilities were pulled outward as rail and water transportation gave way to truck transport, which more easily accommodated remote manufacturing sites. In the suburbs, moreover, managers could secure sufficient land on which to build campus-like offices with low-rise buildings in which they deemed that their employees could interact more conveniently and productively than when they were located on many relatively isolated floors of a downtown skyscraper.

Enterprises also began moving to the new edge cities to shorten employee commutes and better compete for the best-educated talent to fill their high-skill workforce requirements. These people tended, more often than not, to be suburbanites, most of them women. Nearly two-thirds of the increase in civilian employment since 1950 was accounted for by women. Perhaps coincidentally, these factors favoring relocation to the suburbs meshed with the desire on the part of many executives to shorten their own work commutes.

Segregation

Segregation was not a necessary concomitant of sprawl. Urban sprawl is a worldwide phenomenon, but in America more than anywhere else, sprawl was accompanied by residential segregation on a grand scale.

Starting in the 1940s and continuing until 1970, five million blacks migrated from the rural South to the urban North, spurring the white migration from central city to suburbs. The black migration was largely caused by the mechanization of the cotton fields, the booming labor markets in the North with the advent of World War II, and the ending of legal segregation.

Between 1950 and 1970, the percentage of blacks in Chicago went from 14 to 36 percent. In a few short years, the population of vast areas of Chicago's south and west sides became virtually all black. According to Douglas Massey and Nancy Denton, typical inhabitants of today's black urban ghetto are "not only unlikely to come into contact with whites within the particular neighborhood where they live; even if they traveled to the adjacent neighborhood they would still be unlikely to see a white face; and if they went to the next neighborhood beyond that, no whites would be there either. People growing up in such an environment have little direct experience with the culture, norms, and behaviors of the rest of American society and few social contacts with members of other racial groups. Ironically, within a large, diverse, and highly mobile post-industrial society such as the United States, blacks living in the heart of the ghetto are among the most isolated people on earth" (*American Apartheid,* 1993).

Residential segregation is a matter of income as well as race, and the degree of segregation by income is on the increase. At one end of the spectrum are the urban poor. Urban poverty today is fundamentally different from what it was in the past. For one thing, even though the poor had always lived in older, shabbier houses, they at least shared schools and other public facilities with higher-income groups. And the great majority of the poor lived in rural areas. According to William Julius Wilson, "In 1959, only 27 percent of the poverty population in the United States lived in metropolitan central cities. By 1991, the central cities included 43 percent of the nation's poor. The proportion of poor black Americans living in central cities rose even more sharply, from 38 percent in 1959 to 80 percent in 1991. . . . Some of the most rapid increases in concentrated poverty have occurred in African-American neighborhoods" (*When Work Disappears,* 1996).

Between 1970 and 1990, while the black population in the City of Chicago stayed about the same, the non-Hispanic white population declined by about a million. High-density black communities were depopulated. By 1990, the populations of black communities such as East and West Garfield Parks, North Lawndale, Grand Boulevard, Washington Park, and Woodlawn stood at half or less of their 1970 populations. The blacks who left these areas tended to be working- and middle-class families. The result was a substantial reduction in the economic, social, and political resources that make a community vibrant. And the increased social isolation of poor ghetto blacks reduced their chances of acquiring employable skills.

In 1989, the average per capita income of residents in the three richest neighborhoods of Chicago (Lincoln Park, the Loop, and the Near North) was about ten times that of the residents in the three poorest neighborhoods (Grand Boulevard, Riverdale, and Oakland), almost double the multiple for 1979. Likewise, in 1989, the average per capita income of the three richest suburbs (Glencoe, Kenilworth, and Winnetka) was about ten times that of the residents of the three poorest suburbs (Ford Heights, Harvey, and Robbins), up from a multiple of five for 1979. Finally, between 1979 and 1989, the average per capita income of the three richest suburbs, as a multiple of that of the three poorest neighborhoods in Chicago, increased from eight to fifteen.

Income segregation by neighborhood has been accompanied more recently by the private and usually gated residential community, governed by "a thicket of covenants, codes and restrictions. By some estimates nearly four million Americans live in these closed-off, gated communities. About 28 million live in an area governed by a private community association, . . . and that number is expected to double in the next decade." Americans (mostly the rich and the retired) have long had such communities. A September 3, 1995, *New York Times* article observed that "what is different now is that a big portion of middle-class families, in non-retirement, largely white areas of the country, have chosen to wall themselves off, opting for private government, schools and police." The article cited Gerald

Frug, a professor of local government at the Harvard Law School, for his observation that these new private communities are unlike anything America has ever seen. According to Frug, "The village was open to the public [and] did not have these kinds of restrictions. These private communities are totally devoid of random encounters. So you develop this instinct that everyone is just like me, and then you become less likely to support schools, parks or roads for everyone else."

There is much more information for poverty concentration and racial and income segregation than for age segregation. Intuitively, however, it seems that there has been a long-term trend toward residential patterns based on age. For example, many retirement cities attract older people on the promise that their taxes will be used for the kind of facilities they want, not for schools and playgrounds. Do young professionals also tend to congregate in certain urban neighborhoods, such as Lincoln Park in Chicago, where retailers can better cater to their special needs and desires? As a result (partly) of the self-interested choices of empty nesters and young unmarrieds, do the suburbs wind up being the dominant preserve of child-rearing families?

THE ROLE OF TECHNOLOGY

Communications, computer, and other technologies globalized the economic order, and they greatly reduced the need for both manufacturing and supervisory personnel. They also facilitated the outsourcing of operations involving low-skill labor to foreign countries with lower wage scales and more favorable regulatory climates. Moreover, lean production systems brought about substantial improvements in worker productivity.

These developments help explain the sharp downsizings of the nation's largest corporations, and they partly explain why hundreds of corporate employers relocated their principal operations from the central city to the suburbs, where most of the high-skill employees now live. The decline of domestic manufacturing, the suburbanization of employment, and the rise of the low-wage service sector reduced the number of central-city jobs that paid wages sufficient to support a family.

THE ROLE OF PUBLIC POLICY

The role of the FHA in facilitating metropolitan sprawl has been noted. Its programs also hastened the decay of inner-city neighborhoods where loans for repair of existing structures were small and for short terms and at higher interest rates. The FHA's neighborhood evaluation guidelines placed high priority on economic stability and protection from adverse influences, and they warned against crowded neighborhoods, those in transition to lower class occupancy, and those composed of inharmonious racial or nationality groups. And they prohibited guaranties respecting a residential building that was also to be used as a store, an office, or a rental unit. It was not until 1966, following the civil rights legislation, that the FHA drastically changed its policies to make more mortgage insurance available for inner-city neighborhoods. The ironic result of this change "was to increase the speed with which areas went through racial transformation and to victimize those it was designed to help" (Kenneth T. Jackson, *Crabgrass Frontier,* 1985).

More important, the Public Housing Act of 1949 instituted and funded the urban renewal program designed to eradicate urban slums. Since suburban communities refused to permit the construction of public housing, public housing units were overwhelmingly concentrated in the overcrowded and deteriorating inner-city ghettos—the poorest and least socially organized sections of the city and the metropolitan area.

Moreover, while the civil rights legislation of the 1960s enhanced the life chances of better educated minorities, who moved out of the ghettos, it did nothing to improve the lot of the disadvantaged. Rather, the ghetto underclass was deprived of its leaders and role models, and the stability of churches and other community institutions in the inner city was undermined.

Finally, state governance structures and local tax and zoning policies facilitated both the separation of land uses by type and the creation of new school districts and villages differentiated by race and income. Severe restrictions on annexation authority made it politically impossible for central cities in the Northeast and Midwest to expand their territories. Rather, state laws facilitated fragmentation of authority over land use and local taxation among hundreds of small, legally separate units whose officials were motivated to look after the interests of the local community, not those of the larger region. Each unit was free to adopt zoning policies to keep out low-cost housing and other uses that would be a drain on local property tax revenues.

The ultimate example of government fragmentation is Illinois, which has over 6,800 local governments—about 1,400 more than the next closest state, Pennsylvania. Metropolitan Chicago (the six-county area) has nearly 1,300 local governments, including 270 cities and villages, 313 school districts, and over 500 special districts.

CULTURAL FACTORS

The nation has made great progress over the last half century in reducing racial and ethnic discrimination in the realms of employment and public accommodations. It has made little or no such progress over this period in the realm of the neighborhood. This is despite the myriad of Supreme Court decisions and federal, state, and local mandates against residential and school segregation. The tolerance of most whites for racially mixed communities is quite limited. Their apprehensions are associated with the belief that having black neighbors undermines property values and reduces neighborhood safety and morality.

More generally, Americans have long felt the pull of two very different ideologies: that of self-realization in a market economy, and that of community in an egalitarian society. As noted by Alan Altshuler, professor at Harvard's Kennedy School of Government, the norms of egalitarianism have become much more prominent in our public life in recent decades. However, this has made people less willing to live cheek by jowl with people who are very different from themselves. In earlier times one could achieve social differentiation even in the same household, and it was clear to all parties what that social distance was to be. Now, to achieve the same objective one must put physical space between oneself and those who are different. The desire to escape from uncomfortable diversity has been reinforced by the increased fear of crime across racial and other lines.

Yet, as Altshuler says, people don't wish to live without some sense of community; so they look for middle paths. The key to blazing these new paths has been fragmented local government (and, more recently, the gated, privatized community) whereby people having similar socioeconomic characteristics can pool assets to provide collective facilities and services. In this way they need not trigger a level of egalitarianism that would be a drain on their pocketbooks.

METROPOLIS 2020
PROJECT COMMITTEES

Committee Chair, Vice Chairs

ECONOMIC DEVELOPMENT	Michael H. Moskow, Edward J. Noha, Thomas C. Theobald
EDUCATION	Adele S. Simmons
GOVERNANCE	Tyrone C. Fahner, Calvin A. Campbell, Jr., John D. Nichols
LAND USE AND HOUSING	Charles H. Shaw, William M. Goodyear, Lawrence F. Levy
TAXATION	James R. Kackley, Michael L. Murphy, Richard P. Toft
TRANSPORTATION	Jerry Pearlman, Frank W. Considine, Daniel R. Toll
STEERING COMMITTEE	John M. Madigan, Chairman of the Commercial Club of Chicago
	Richard L. Thomas, Chairman of the Civic Committee of the Club
	Arnold R. Weber, President of the Club
	Elmer W. Johnson, Project Director
	Tyrone C. Fahner, James R. Kackley, Michael H. Moskow,
	Jerry Pearlman, Charles H. Shaw, Adele S. Simmons, chairs of the
	six working committees, and George A. Ranney, Jr., chair of the
	strategy committee
EDITORIAL BOARD	Richard G. Cline, Tyrone C. Fahner, Richard J. Franke, Elmer W.
	Johnson, James R. Kackley, R. Eden Martin, Michael H. Moskow,
	Michael E. Murphy, Jerry Pearlman, Donald S. Perkins, George A.
	Ranney, Jr., John M. Richman, Charles H. Shaw, Adele S. Simmons,
	Richard P. Toft, and Arnold R. Weber

N O T E S

INTRODUCTION

1. One could argue that metropolitan Chicago should be defined to comprehend a much larger area. This is especially true, for example, in the area of transportation planning. Moreover, the federal Office of Management and Budget articulated a new set of urban classifications following the 1990 census. Under the new definitions, Chicago-Gary-Kenosha constitutes the third largest Consolidated Metropolitan Statistical Area (CMSA) in the United States. The criteria for determining a CMSA (there are nineteen CMSAs in the United States) include population density, population growth patterns, contiguity of counties, degree of urbanization, and commuting patterns. The Chicago CMSA consists of the NIPC six-county area, plus DeKalb, Grundy, Kankakee, and Kendall Counties in Illinois; Lake and Porter Counties in Indiana; and Kenosha County in Wisconsin.

The Chicago CMSA has about twice the geographic territory of the NIPC area but has a population that is only about 12 or 13 percent larger. The Commercial Club determined early on in the project that it should use the NIPC definition of metropolitan Chicago for several reasons: useful data is more readily available over a longer period of time; the intensity of economic and social interaction among people in the six-county area is much higher than it is in the larger CMSA; and in the implementation process, the Club will have its hands full without calling for tristate cooperation. Nevertheless, the Club recognizes that some of the recommendations in the plan will need to be reconsidered from time to time in light of the dynamic nature of transportation and land-use patterns in the larger tristate metropolitan area.

2. NIPC has forecast that the metropolitan population will grow from 7.7 million in 1998 to 9.2 million in 2020. Hispanics are projected to account for close to two-thirds of the increase, and blacks for almost a third. Asians will account for most of the balance, and the white population will remain about the same.

3. Burnham understood that "the essence of a city is concentration, and concentration requires focal points, nodes of attention, monuments. . . . [The Plan was] designed to . . . maintain hopes that were unachievable within a single lifetime." From a speech to the Commercial Club of Chicago by Neil Harris, pro-

fessor of history at the University of Chicago, given in 1979 on the occasion of the seventieth anniversary of the Burnham Plan.

4. The report of that effort, "Jobs for Metropolitan Chicago," described the challenge of that day. For thirty consecutive years, metropolitan Chicago had experienced a declining share of the national job market. The study led to the creation of the Club's Civic Committee. That committee's subsequent contributions to improvements in the efficiency and effectiveness of local governments and of public schools and its efforts to enhance research and development in higher technology have helped build the underpinnings for the job growth that the region has since enjoyed.

5. These three museums are part of a larger consortium of "Museums in the Park," including the Art Institute of Chicago, the Museum of Science and Industry, the DuSable Museum of African-American History, the Mexican Fine Arts Center Museum, the Chicago Academy of Sciences, and the Chicago Historical Society. Each of these museums receives a portion of its funds from the Chicago Park District (via its property tax levy). There are few other cities that can match this combined cultural and educational resource. Their impact on cultural tourism is substantial. According to a recent Arts Council report, the major museums are far more important than sports events as a driver of tourism. These institutions also exert an enormous influence in the education of children who visit the museums both with their families and as part of organized school groups. We are also beginning to see the potential of these museums in enriching the curricula of elementary and secondary public and private schools.

6. "The Next Agenda for America's Cities: Competing in a Global Economy," the keynote address given on June 24, 1997, at the James W. Rouse Forum on the American City, included in an executive summary on that forum (Washington, D.C.: Fannie Mae Foundation, 1997). For an excellent review of the literature on the influence of communications technologies on the shape and form of metropolitan regions, see "Technology and Cities," by Mitchell L. Moss, in *Cityscape: A Journal of Policy Development and Research,* vol. 3, no. 3 (a publication of the U.S. Department of Housing and Urban Development's Office of Policy Development and Research, 1998). Mr. Moss is professor of urban policy and planning at New York University.

C H A P T E R   O N E

1. See Robert B. Downs, *Horace Mann: Champion of Public Schools* (New York: Twayne Publishers, 1974), 110ff. A century and a half after Mann's findings, a great economist observed that the most important achievement of modern economic growth is undoubtedly the increase in the stock of human capital: "The development and transmission of practical knowledge and intellectual skills are at the heart of economic development." Theodore W. Schultz, *Investing in People: The Economics of Population Quality* (Berkeley: University of California Press, 1981), 47.

2. *Economist,* March 29, 1997, 21–23.

3. See chapter 7 ("Major Lessons from the Initiating Phase of Chicago School Reform") of an excellent book by Anthony S. Bryk, Penny Bender Sebring, David Kerbow, Sharon Rollow, and John Q. Easton, *Charting Chicago School Reform: Democratic Localism as a Lever for Change* (Boulder, Colo.: Westview Press, 1999).

4. Of the many outstanding civic organizations that worked to bring about the 1997 amendments, none deserves more credit for the teacher certification reforms than Chicago United, Inc., a diversified corporate membership organization whose mission is to improve race relations through education and economic development.

5. Illinois *Revised Statutes,* chapter 105.

6. The statements quoted in this paragraph are from pages 4–7 of *Rising to the Challenge: The Future of Illinois Teachers* (August 1996), prepared by the University of Illinois at Chicago and the Illinois State Board of Education Task Force on Teacher Preparation, Certification, and Professional Development.

7. The capacity for such care is grossly inadequate to meet present needs, and it will have to be greatly expanded as "welfare-to-work" policies are implemented.

8. See, for example, the unpublished paper by G. Alfred Hess, Jr., professor at Northwestern University,

entitled "Education Reform Policy in Illinois: Problems, Conundrums, and Strategies" (winter 1998), prepared for the Chicago Assembly.

9. Ibid.

10. Richard F. Elmore. "Accountability in Local School Districts: Learning to Do the Right Things," 1996, unpublished paper prepared for a symposium at the University of Illinois at Urbana-Champaign, October 16–17, 1997. Some excellent reports have been issued in recent years on teacher recruitment, preparation, and professional development. See, especially, *What Matters Most: Teaching for America's Future,* September 1996, a report of the National Commission on Teaching and America's Future; and the task-force report referred to in note 6 above.

CHAPTER TWO

1. Nearly 64 percent of the region's lane miles are under the jurisdiction of municipalities, counties, and townships, but that 64 percent accounts for only 37 percent of vehicle travel. The other 63 percent of vehicle travel is handled by state roads (freeways, tollways, and arterial roads, which account for 36 percent of lane miles in the region).

2. *Cities in Civilization* (New York: Pantheon Books, 1998), 964–965.

CHAPTER THREE

1. *New Visions for Metropolitan America* (Washington, D.C.: Brookings Institution), 1994.

2. James E. Frank, *The Costs of Alternative Development Patterns: A Review of the Literature* (Washington, D.C.: Urban Land Institute), 1989.

3. Some of the most rapid increases in concentrated poverty have occurred in African American neighborhoods in the central city. Of the ten community areas that represent the historic core of Chicago's Black Belt, eight had rates of poverty in 1990 that exceeded 45 percent, including three with rates higher than 50 percent and three that surpassed 60 percent. In 1970, only two of these neighborhoods had poverty rates above 40 percent.

CHAPTER FOUR

1. In Burnham's famous Plan of Chicago, he laid out an elaborate scheme of highways and roads for the entire region. As to implementation, "pending the creation of a metropolitan commission for the treatment of the entire area," he advocated a process of intergovernmental cooperation!

2. George A. Berman, "Taking Subsidiarity Seriously: Federalism in the European Community and the United States," in *Columbia Law Review* 94 (1994): 331, 338.

3. By contrast, the portion of state income taxes and motor fuel taxes that goes back to municipalities is distributed in the form of revenue sharing on a per capita basis.

4. For a fuller description of these criteria, see the excellent article by J. Fred Giertz, Therese J. McGuire, and James D. Nowlan, "State and Local Revenue Sources in Illinois," in *Dilemmas of Fiscal Reform: Paying for State and Local Government in Illinois,* L. B. Joseph, ed. (Chicago: Center for Urban Research and Policy Studies, University of Chicago, 1996).

5. Glenn W. Fisher, *The Worst Tax? A History of the Property Tax in America* (Lawrence: University Press of Kansas, 1996), 120.

6. While these are the percentages that Cook purports to use, in practice it values all categories of properties at still lower percentages of market value, on average, thus requiring a high state equalization factor.

7. Fisher, *The Worst Tax?* p. 209, note 27.

CHAPTER FIVE

1. Over the last few years, the Illinois Community College System has developed a "Workforce Preparation Action Plan." One of the initiatives under this plan (termed "Education to Careers") calls for state and local partnerships of business, labor, and education to prepare young people with the basic academic and technical skills needed for careers in skilled and profitable jobs. The program includes school-based learning and career counseling, work experiences integrated with educational programs, and activities that connect educators and employers. These and other initiatives under the plan are in the early stages of operation, and they should be monitored by Metropolis 2020 to assess their effectiveness.

2. See the excellent report by Patricia Widmayer and Gary Greenberg, "Putting Our Minds Together: The Digital Network Infrastructure and Metropolitan Chicago," a report for the Metropolitan Planning Council (Evanston: Northwestern University, September 1998).

3. "The Next Agenda for America's Cities: Competing in a Global Economy," the keynote address given on June 24, 1997, at the James W. Rouse Forum on the American City, included in an executive summary on that forum (Washington, D.C.: Fannie Mae Foundation, 1997).

CHAPTER SIX

1. Robert B. Downs, *Horace Mann: Champion of Public Schools* (New York: Twayne Publishers, 1974), 38ff.

2. In late 1997, several business and civic organizations teamed up with the Chicago Public School System and the Chicago Principals and Administrators Association to launch two new initiatives. One is LAUNCH, which stands for Leadership Academy: An Urban Network for Chicago. It is the first big-city effort to recruit and train principals. Under the program, forty teachers, assistant principals, and other educators were selected for a six-week program in management and budget training conducted in the summer of 1998 at Northwestern University. Martin J. Koldyke, a member of the Commercial Club, is a cofounder of this initiative. The second is PENCUL, which stands for Partnership to Encourage the Next Century's Urban Leaders. Under PENCUL, a new Chicago Principal Assessment Center provides aspiring principals a series of interviews, exercises, and group activities to simulate the principal's duties over a one-day period. That program will also maintain a database of principal candidates for local school councils and offer free training to 100 councils on how to select a principal.

3. For a description of these two boards and the standards they have developed, see *What Matters Most: Teaching for America's Future,* September 1996, a report of the National Commission on Teaching and America's Future.

4. Irving B. Harris, *Children in Jeopardy: Can We Break the Cycle of Poverty?* (New Haven: Yale Child Study Center, 1996). Mr. Harris, a long-time member of the Commercial Club, focuses on the first several weeks and months of a child's life in which the quality of care and nurture it receives makes a critical difference in its life chances.

CHAPTER SEVEN

1. Three excellent reports focus mainly on the employment and training needs of the disadvantaged living in Chicago. One is "Levers for Change: Revisiting 'Systemic Changes for Employment and Training in Chicago,'" a report to the MacArthur Foundation prepared by the Council for Adult and Experiential Learning, April 21, 1997. The second is a report of the Workforce Development Project written by Joan Fitzgerald and Davis Jenkins of the Great Cities Institute, University of Illinois at Chicago, "Making Workforce Development Work for the Urban Core," January 1998. The third is "Five Stops on the Road to Improving Chicago's One-Stops," a report of the Chicago Jobs Council, April 1998.

2. "The Next Agenda for America's Cities: Competing in a Global Economy," the keynote address given

on June 24, 1997, at the James W. Rouse Forum on the American City, included in an executive summary on that forum (Washington, D.C.: Fannie Mae Foundation, 1997).

3. The Illinois Coalition is a private-public partnership dedicated to strengthening Illinois' economy through science and technology. For a full description of the proposal described in the text, see "The Chicago Technology Growth Fund," a concept paper by the Illinois Coalition, dated June 1998.

4. As part of these efforts, the city commissioned a study by Arthur Andersen's Real Estate Advisory Services Group to conduct an industrial market and strategic analysis. Its report, dated March 1998, indicates that from 1990 to 1995, the city's occupied industrial space (which includes space used as manufacturing operations, distribution facilities, and flex/service operations) declined from 175.8 to 150.7 million square feet. Over the same period, occupied industrial space in the rest of the region grew moderately from 552.6 to 573.5 million square feet. Nevertheless, the report projects that between 1997 and 2005, the city has the opportunity to add 14 or 15 million new square feet of such space.

5. See the recent, but undated, report of the City's Department of Planning and Development, entitled "Proposed Industrial Redevelopment Project Areas: Tax Increment Financing Program." Also see *Assessing the Impact of Tax Increment Financing in Northeastern Illinois,* a March 1997 report of the Civic Federation.

6. These are just some of the opportunities identified in an excellent pro bono study recently conducted by the Chicago office of the Boston Consulting Group in conjunction with and on behalf of the Initiative for a Competitive Inner City (ICIC, a nonprofit organization founded by Michael Porter, professor at the Harvard Business School). The findings and recommendations of this study are set forth in a report dated February 1998. The task force referred to in the text will be working with the city and various nonprofit organizations to exploit the opportunities for creating wealth in these neighborhoods.

7. An excellent example is the Cambridge Technology Group, a private company located on the campus of the Massachusetts Institute of Technology.

CHAPTER EIGHT

1. These forecasts were recently prepared as a basis for testing and justifying the 2020 RTP (CATS' regional transportation plan, discussed in chapter 2). The numbers endorsed by NIPC reflect both municipal and county input, and they reinforce a policy of effectively encouraging infill and redevelopment while deterring sprawl.

CHAPTER NINE

1. Anthony Downs, *New Visions for Metropolitan America* (Washington, D.C.: Brookings Institution, 1994), 106–107.

2. To be eligible, individuals must have incomes equal to or below 60 percent of the area's median income.

3. Account holders have two years to accumulate at least $600, which will be matched 2:1 up to $1,200.

4. Administered by the Office of the Comptroller of the Currency, Administrator of National Banks.

5. Suburban centers that have specialized in housing counseling for African Americans and other minorities include Hope Fair Housing Center, South Suburban Housing Center, Housing Coalition of the Southern Suburbs, Interfaith Housing Center of the Northern Suburbs, Fair Housing Center of Lake County, and the Oak Park Regional Housing Center.

CHAPTER TEN

1. At present, the State of Illinois raises $205 per car annually from fuel taxes and registration fees. Adding in local fuel taxes (5 cents in Chicago and 6 cents in Cook County), even though these taxes are not dedicated

Economist. "A Survey of Cities." July 29, 1995.

Garreau, Joel. *Edge City: Life on the New Frontier.* New York: Doubleday, 1991.

Heenan, David A. *The New Corporate Frontier: The Big Move to Small Town, USA.* New York: McGraw-Hill, 1991.

Newsweek. "Bye-Bye, Suburban Dream." May 15, 1995.

Peirce, Neal R. *Citistates: How Urban America Can Prosper in a Competitive World.* Washington, D.C.: Seven Locks Press, 1993.

Summers, Anita A., Paul C. Cheshire, and Lanfranco Senn, eds. *Urban Change in the United States and Western Europe: Comparative Analysis and Policy.* Washington, D.C.: Urban Institute Press, 1993.

Yaro, Robert D., and Tony Hiss. *A Region at Risk: The Third Regional Plan for the New York–New Jersey–Connecticut Metropolitan Area.* Washington, D.C.: Island Press, 1995.

HISTORICAL, POLITICAL, AND/OR SOCIOLOGICAL STUDIES

Banham, Reyner. *Los Angeles: The Architecture of Four Ecologies.* London: Penguin Books, 1971.

Burgess, Ernest W., ed. *The Urban Community: Selected Papers from the Proceedings of the American Sociological Society, 1925.* Chicago: University of Chicago Press, 1926.

Cities. A Scientific American *Book.* New York: Alfred A. Knopf, 1965.

Ehrenhalt, Alan. *The Lost City: The Forgotten Virtues of Community in America.* New York: Basic Books, 1995.

Exploding Metropolis, The. Articles selected by the editors of *Fortune.* Garden City, N.Y.: Doubleday, 1958.

Fishman, Robert. *Bourgeois Utopias: The Rise and Fall of Suburbia.* New York: Basic Books, 1987.

——. "Megalopolis Unbound." *Wilson Quarterly* (winter 1990): 25–48.

Girouard, Mark. *Cities and People: A Social and Architectural History.* New Haven: Yale University Press, 1985.

Goodman, Paul, and Percival Goodman. *Communitas: Means of Livelihood and Ways of Life.* Chicago: University of Chicago Press, 1947.

Hall, Peter. *The World Cities.* New York: McGraw-Hill, 1966.

——. *Cities of Tomorrow: An Intellectual History of Urban Planning and Design in the Twentieth Century.* Cambridge, U.K.: Blackwell, 1988.

——. *Cities in Civilization.* New York: Pantheon Books, 1998.

Haworth, Lawrence. *The Good City.* Bloomington: Indiana University Press, 1963; Westport, Conn.: Greenwood Press, 1990.

Jackson, Kenneth T. *Crabgrass Frontier: The Suburbanization of the United States.* New York: Oxford University Press, 1985.

Jacobs, Jane. *The Economy of Cities.* New York: Random House, 1969.

——. *Cities and the Wealth of Nations: Principles of Economic Life.* New York: Random House, 1984.

Mumford, Lewis. *The Culture of Cities.* New York: Harcourt Brace Jovanovich, 1938.

——. *From the Ground Up: Observations on Contemporary Architecture, Housing, Highway Building, and Civic Design.* Harcourt Brace Jovanovich, 1956.

——. *The City in History: Its Origins, Its Transformations, and Its Prospects.* Harcourt Brace Jovanovich, 1961.

——. *The Highway and the City.* Harcourt Brace Jovanovich, 1963.

Perry, Clarence Arthur. "The Neighborhood Unit: A Scheme of Arrangement for the Family-Life Community." Published by the Committee on Regional Plan of New York and Its Environs, New York, and issued as vol. 7 of its regional survey, 1929. Reprinted in 1974 by Arno Press Inc., a New York Times Company.

Rybczynski, Witold. *City Life: Urban Expectations in a New World.* New York: Scribner, 1995.

Weber, Max. *The City.* 1921. Reprint, New York: Free Press, 1958.

Wiebe, Robert H. *The Segmented Society: An Introduction to the Meaning of America.* New York: Oxford University Press, 1975.

LAND USE, HOUSING, AND THE ENVIRONMENT

"Beyond Sprawl: New Patterns of Growth to Fit the New California." 1995. A report sponsored by Bank America Corporation and three other organizations calling for managing growth in California in order to improve the state's competitiveness and quality of life. Much of the basic research behind the report was prepared by Steven Moss and his associates at the consulting firm of M. Cubed, which produced a much longer working paper in June 1994 entitled "California at a Cross-Roads: The Costs of Sprawling Land Use Patterns."

Blakely, Edward J., and Mary Gail Snyder. *Fortress America: Gated Communities in the United States.* Washington, D.C.: Brookings Institution Press, 1997.

Bosselman, Fred P. "The Commodification of Nature's Metropolis: The Historical Context of Illinois' Unique Zoning Standards" *Northern Illinois University Law Review* 12, no. 3 (summer 1992); see also, in the same issue, a series of articles as part of a symposium on "What's Wrong with Illinois Land Use Law?"

Diamond, Henry L., and Patrick F. Noonan. 1996. *Land Use in America.* Washington, D.C.: Island Press, 1996.

Metropolitan Planning Council. *Housing for a Competitive Region, December 1995.* Chicago: Metropolitan Planning Council, 1995.

Moe, Richard, and Carter Wilkie. *Changing Places: Rebuilding Community in the Age of Sprawl.* New York: Henry Holt and Company, 1997.

Real Estate Research Corporation. *The Costs of Sprawl: Environmental and Economic Costs of Alternative Residential Development Patterns at the Urban Fringe.* A detailed cost analysis prepared for the Council on Environmental Quality; the Office of Policy Development and Research, Department of Housing and Urban Development; and the Office of Planning and Management, Environmental Protection Agency. Washington, D.C.: U.S. Government Printing Office, 1974.

URBAN TRANSPORTATION

Altshuler, Alan, John R. Pucher, and James Womack. *The Urban Transportation Problem: Politics and Policy Innovation.* Cambridge, Mass.: MIT Press, 1979.

Bottles, Scott L. *Los Angeles and the Automobile: The Making of the Modern City.* Berkeley: University of California Press, 1987.

Calthorpe Associates. *Transit-Oriented Development Design Guidelines.* Sacramento, Calif.: Calthorpe Associates, November 1990.

Downs, Anthony. *Stuck in Traffic: Coping with Peak-Hour Traffic Congestion.* Washington, D.C.: Brookings Institution; Cambridge, Mass.: Lincoln Institute of Land Policy, 1992.

Johnson, Elmer W. *Avoiding the Collision of Cities and Cars.* Cambridge, Mass.: American Academy of Arts and Sciences, 1993.

Lave, Charles, ed. *Urban Transit: The Private Challenge to Public Transportation.* New York: Ballinger Publishing, 1984.

Meyer, John. Presentation at a seminar in Berlin on urban transportation policy, sponsored by the Aspen Institute, May 1992.

Meyer, John, and José A. Gómez-Ibáñez. *Autos, Transit, and Cities.* Cambridge, Mass.: Harvard University Press, 1981.

Mumford, Lewis. *The Highway and the City.* New York: New American Library, 1964.

Pucher, John. "Urban Travel Behavior as the Outcome of Public Policy: The Example of Modal-Split in Western Europe and North America." *Journal of the American Planning Association* 54 (autumn 1988): 509–520.

Thomson, J. Michael. *Great Cities and Their Traffic.* New York: Penguin Books, 1977.

Warner, Sam Bass, Jr. *Streetcar Suburbs: The Process of Growth in Boston, 1870–1900.* Cambridge, Mass.: Harvard University Press and MIT Press, 1962.

———. *The Urban Wilderness: A History of the American City.* New York: Random House, 1972.

Weiner, Edward. *Urban Transportation Planning in the United States: An Historical Overview.* Washington, D.C.: U.S. Department of Transportation, 1992.

Wormser, Lisa. "Design for Living: Can Road Standards Respond to a Sense of Place?" *Surface Transportation Policy Project Bulletin* 2, no. 1 (November 1992).

REGIONALISM AND GOVERNANCE

Altshuler, Alan A. *The Governance of Urban Land: Critical Issues and Research Priorities.* Faculty Research Working Paper Series. Cambridge, Mass: Harvard University, John F. Kennedy School of Government, 1993.

Altshuler, Alan A., William Morrill, Harold Wolman, and Faith Mitchell, eds. *Governance and Opportunity in Metropolitan America.* National Research Council. Committee on Improving the Future of U.S. Cities through Improved Metropolitan Area Governance. Washington, D.C.: National Academy Press, 1999.

Briffault, Richard. "Our Localism: Part I—The Structure of Local Government Law," and "Our Localism: Part II—Localism and Legal Theory." *Columbia Law Review* 90 (1990): 1–115 and 346–454.

Cisneros, Henry. *Regionalism: The New Geography of Opportunity.* Washington, D.C.: U.S. Department of Housing and Urban Development, March 1995.

Dodge, William R. *Regional Excellence: Governing Together to Compete Globally and Flourish Locally.* Washington, D.C.: National League of Cities, 1996.

Gove, Samuel K., and James D. Nowlan. *Illinois Politics and Government: The Expanding Metropolitan Frontier.* Lincoln: University of Nebraska Press, 1996.

Rothblatt, Donald N., and Andrew Sancton, eds. *Metropolitan Governance: American/Canadian Intergovernmental Perspectives.* Berkeley: Institute of Governmental Studies Press, University of California, Berkeley; Kingston, Ont.: Institute of Intergovernmental Relations, Queen's University, 1993.

Rusk, David. *Cities Without Suburbs.* Washington, D.C.: Woodrow Wilson Center Press, 1993.

———. *Inside Game/Outside Game: Winning Strategies for Saving Urban America.* Washington, D.C.: Brookings Institution, 1999.

Savitch, H. V., et al. "Ties That Bind: Central Cities, Suburbs, and the New Metropolitan Region." *Economic Development Quarterly* (November 1993).

Stone, Deborah C. "Creating a Regional Community: The Case for Regional Cooperation." A report of the Metropolitan Planning Council's Regional Cooperation Initiative, Chicago, Illinois, 1995.

Voith, Richard P. "City and Suburban Growth: Substitutes or Complements?" Federal Reserve Bank of Philadelphia, *Business Review* (September/October 1992).

FISCAL POLICY AND ECONOMIC STRATEGIES

Altshuler, Alan A., and José A. Gómez-Ibáñez. *Regulation for Revenue: The Political Economy of Land Use Exactions.* Washington, D.C.: Brookings Institution; Cambridge, Mass.: Lincoln Institute of Land Policy, 1993.

"America's New Economy and the Challenge of the Cities." A HUD Report on Metropolitan Economic Strategy. U.S. Department of Housing and Urban Development, October 1996.

Dilemmas of Fiscal Reform: Paying for State and Local Government in Illinois. Edited by Lawrence B. Joseph. A Chicago Assembly Book. Chicago: Center for Urban Research and Policy Studies, University of Chicago, 1996.

Fisher, Glen W. *The Worst Tax? A History of the Property Tax in America.* Lawrence: University Press of Kansas, 1996.

Orfield, Myron. *Metropolitics: A Regional Agenda for Community and Stability.* Washington, D.C.: Brookings Institution; Cambridge, Mass.: Lincoln Institute of Land Policy, 1997.

Porter, Michael E. "The Competitive Advantage of the Inner City." *Harvard Business Review* (May–June 1995): 55–71.

———. "The Next Agenda for America's Cities: Competing in a Global Economy." First Annual James W. Rouse Lecture. Washington, D.C.: Fannie Mae Foundation, 1997.

Reuss, Henry S. *Revenue-Sharing: Crutch or Catalyst for State and Local Governments?* New York: Praeger Publishers, 1970.

———. *To Save Our Cities: What Needs to Be Done.* Washington, D.C.: Public Affairs Press, 1977.

Sassen, Saskia. *The Global City: New York, London, Tokyo.* Princeton: Princeton University Press, 1991.

———. *Cities in a World Economy.* Thousand Oaks, Calif.: Pine Forge Press, 1994.

URBAN DESIGN AND STRUCTURE

Barnett, Jonathan. *The Elusive City: Five Centuries of Design, Ambition, and Miscalculation.* New York: Harper and Row, 1986.

Bendixson, Terence. *European Cities.* Brussels: Association des Constructeurs Européens d'Automobiles, 1994.

Calthorpe, Peter. *The Next American Metropolis: Ecology, Community, and the American Dream.* New York: Princeton Architectural Press, 1993.

Howard, Ebenezer. *Garden Cities of Tomorrow.* 1898. Cambridge, Mass.: MIT Press, 1965.

Jacobs, Jane. *The Death and Life of Great American Cities.* New York: Random House, 1961.

Katz, Peter. *The New Urbanism: Toward an Architecture of Community.* With an afterword by Vincent Scully. New York: McGraw-Hill, 1994.

Kemmis, Daniel. *The Good City and the Good Life.* Boston: Houghton Mifflin, 1995.

Kivell, Philip. *Land and the City: Patterns and Processes of Urban Change.* London: Routledge, 1993.

Safdie, Moshe. *The City after the Automobile: An Architect's Vision.* New York: Basic Books, 1997.

Venturi, Robert, Denise Scott Brown, Steven Izenour. *Learning from Las Vegas.* Cambridge, Mass.: MIT Press, 1972.

Webber, Melvin M., ed. *Explorations into Urban Structure.* Philadelphia: University of Pennsylvania Press, 1964.

Wright, Frank Lloyd. *The Living City.* New York: New American Library, 1963.

RACE, POVERTY, EDUCATION, AND COMMUNITY

Byrk, Anthony S., Penny Bender Sebring, David Kerbow, Sharon Rollow, and John Q. Easton. *Charting Chicago School Reform: Democratic Localism as a Lever for Change.* Boulder, Colo.: Westview Press, 1999.

Case, Anne C., and Lawrence F. Katz. "The Company You Keep: The Effects of Family and Neighborhood on Disadvantaged Youths." Unpublished working paper no. 3705, prepared for the National Bureau of Economic Research, Cambridge, Mass., 1991.

Cisneros, Henry. *Higher Ground: Faith Communities and Community Building.* Washington, D.C.: U.S. Department of Housing and Urban Development, February 1996.

Committee for Economic Development. *Rebuilding Inner-City Communities: A New Approach to the Nation's Urban Crisis.* A statement by the Research and Policy Committee of the Committee for Economic Development, New York, 1995.

Dash, Leon. *Rosa Lee: A Mother and Her Family in Urban America.* New York: Basic Books, 1996.

Downs, Anthony. *Neighborhoods and Urban Development.* Washington, D.C.: Brookings Institution, 1981.

Empowerment: A New Covenant with America's Communities. First National Urban Policy Report by the U.S. Department of Housing and Urban Development, Office of Policy Development and Research, April 3, 1995.

Haar, Charles. *Suburbs under Siege: Race, Space, and Audacious Judges.* Princeton: Princeton University Press, 1995.

Harris, Irving B. *Children in Jeopardy: Can We Break the Cycle of Poverty?* New Haven: Yale Child Study Center, 1996.

Jargowsky, Paul A. "Take the Money and Run: Economic Segregation in U.S. Metropolitan Areas," working paper, University of Texas at Dallas, School of Social Sciences, undated.

Jencks, Christopher. *Rethinking Social Policy: Race, Poverty, and the Underclass.* Cambridge, Mass.: Harvard University Press, 1992.

Jencks, Christopher, and Paul E. Peterson, eds. *The Urban Underclass.* Washington, D.C.: Brookings Institution, 1991.

Kain, John F. *The Cumulative Impacts of Slavery, Jim Crow, and Housing Market Discrimination on Black Welfare.* Cambridge, Mass.: Lincoln Institute of Land Policy, 1993.

Katz, Michael. *Improving Poor People: The Welfare State, the "Underclass," and Urban Schools as History.* Princeton: Princeton University Press, 1995. See chapter 3, "Urban Schools."

Ladd, Helen, and John Yinger. *America's Ailing Cities: Fiscal Health and the Design of Urban Policy.* Baltimore: Johns Hopkins University Press, 1989.

Lemann, Nicholas. *The Promised Land: The Great Black Migration and How It Changed America.* New York: Alfred A. Knopf, 1991.

———. "The Myth of Community Development." *The New York Times Magazine,* January 4, 1994.

Levy, Frank. "The Future Path and Consequences of U.S. Earnings-Education Gap." Unpublished paper prepared for the Colloquium on U.S. Wage Trends in the 1980s. Federal Reserve Bank of New York, November 3–4, 1994.

Massey, Douglas, and Nancy Denton. *American Apartheid: Segregation and the Making of the Underclass.* Cambridge, Mass.: Harvard University Press, 1993.

McKnight, John. *The Careless Society: Community and Its Counterfeits.* New York: Basic Books, 1995.

Orfield, Gary, and Carole Ashkinaze. *The Closing Door: Conservative Policy and Black Opportunity.* Chicago: University of Chicago Press, 1991.

Peterson, George E., and Wayne Vroman, eds. *Urban Labor Markets and Job Opportunity.* Washington, D.C.: Urban Institute Press, 1992.

Peterson, Paul E. *City Limits.* Chicago: University of Chicago Press, 1981.

———, ed. *The New Urban Reality.* Washington, D.C.: Brookings Institution, 1985.

Plater-Zyberk, Elizabeth. "It Takes a Village to Raise a Child." Discussion paper for a seminar on suburbs and cities held under the auspices of the Aspen Institute in Aspen, Colorado, August 20–24, 1994.

Vergara, Camilo José. *The New American Ghetto.* New Brunswick, N.J.: Rutgers University Press, 1995.

Wilson, William Julius. *The Truly Disadvantaged: The Inner City, the Underclass, and Public Policy.* Chicago: University of Chicago Press, 1987.

———. *When Work Disappears: The World of the New Urban Poor.* New York: Alfred A. Knopf, 1996.

TECHNOLOGY: ITS ECONOMIC, SOCIAL, AND SPATIAL IMPACTS

Buchanan, R. A. *The Power of the Machine: The Impact of Technology from 1700 to the Present.* London: Penguin Books, 1992.

Office of Technology Assessment, Congress of the United States. *The Technological Reshaping of Metropolitan America.* Washington, D.C.: U.S. Government Printing Office, 1995.

Widmayer, Patricia, and Gary Greenberg. "Putting Our Minds Together: The Digital Network Infrastructure and Metropolitan Chicago." A report for the Metropolitan Planning Council. Evanston: Northwestern University, September 1998.

PICTURE CREDITS

INDEX

References to tables and figures are indicated by *t* and *f*, respectively.